Finding the Numinous

Finding the Numinous

An Ecocritical Look at *Dune* and *The Lord of the Rings*

Willow Wilson DiPasquale

The Kent State University Press
KENT, OHIO

© 2025 by The Kent State University Press, Kent, Ohio 44242
All rights reserved
ISBN 978-1-60635-492-6
Published in the United States of America

No part of this book may be used or reproduced, in any manner whatsoever, without written permission from the Publisher, except in the case of short quotations in critical reviews or articles.

Cataloging information for this title is available at the Library of Congress.

29 28 27 26 25   5 4 3 2 1

CONTENTS

Acknowledgments   vii

Introduction   1

1 Mirrors and the Numinous
Mythopoeia, Ecocriticism, and Sacred Nature   5

2 Forests and Deserts
Tolkien's and Herbert's Landscape Descriptions   26

3 Halflings and Harkonnens
How Middle-earth and Dune's Communities Model Environmentalism   58

4 Nature's Voice
Language in the Legendarium and Duniverse   85

5 "To Hold Communion with Living Things"
The Lives and Beliefs of Tolkien and Herbert   114

Conclusion   131

Notes   140

Bibliography   159

Index   163

ACKNOWLEDGMENTS

This book is dedicated to my four sisters. My love of fantasy and science fiction comes directly from them; they shared their reading tastes and their favorite authors with me, especially J. R. R. Tolkien and Frank Herbert. This book is also dedicated to my parents, whose love of literature and knowledge opened the path to my own intellectual pursuits.

Thank you to the late Rev. Dr. James Pain for his remarkable seminars in C. S. Lewis, Charles Williams, and, of course, Tolkien; his wisdom, warmth, and intellect guided many students at Drew University and provided me the opportunity to begin shaping the ideas that became this book. To Dr. Robert Peirano and Dr. Liana Piehler, please accept my gratitude for supervising my dissertation; without your thoughtful, challenging questions and generous advice, this book would not exist.

I would like to thank Dr. Valerie Hanson for reading my manuscript proposal—your reassurance and gentle feedback gave me the confidence to move forward with this project. To Prof. Marie Taylor, thank you for your endless encouragement and wonderfully honest takes on my writing over the past fifteen years. Sharing our writing and teaching experiences has been a professional and personal highlight. Thank you, as well, to Dominic Nardi and Trevor Brierly, whose readerly insights and expertise on Tolkien and Herbert are much appreciated.

At the Kent State University Press, Clara Totten has been so very supportive; thank you for your faith in this book and your help in making it a reality. I am also very grateful to the production team, particularly Valerie Ahwee for her patience and care during the copyedit. My appreciation, too, to Mary Young for her guidance, and Christine Brooks for envisioning the wonderful cover design.

Finally, I am grateful to my husband, Andrew, for nearly fifteen years of support, partnership, and understanding through long days and late nights grading and writing. (And appreciation to my faithful furry companion, Panger-Ban, who has kept me company on many of those late nights.)

INTRODUCTION

At its core, mythopoeia designates the literary act of "myth-making," the creation of a self-referential, purposeful mythology; in J. R. R. Tolkien's view, it is a creative art about "fundamental things." Its function is to bring mythology and its attendant themes and archetypes to modern readers, and thus each mythopoeic work varies in which themes and archetypes it presents. This book explores the premise that the environments depicted in Tolkien's *The Lord of the Rings* (1954–55) and Frank Herbert's *Dune* saga (1965–85) are not only for the purpose of world-building; rather, these imagined worlds' environments are as fundamental to understanding these authors' mythic and perhaps even moral visions as the novels' characters, plots, and themes. While several scholars have examined the topic of environment in these works separately, most comparisons between the two authors' works have been general rather than specific, and none have drawn this sustained comparison of both authors' works at once through the dual lenses of mythopoeia and ecocritical theory.

The environment as depicted in these works, and the characters' relationship to it, underpin the moral philosophy of these two writers, whether explicitly or implicitly. This ecocritical vision is what sets apart Tolkien's and Herbert's particular mythopoeic fiction—their emphasis on concern for and preservation of nature is at the core of their mythologies, suggesting to their readers that such concern and preservation are timeless, innately human desires, and necessary to a spiritually holistic experience, thus reinforcing Tolkien's emphasis on the "fundamental things" mythopoeic fiction explores. By drawing inspiration from prior myths, these writers are able to present their new ideas in a familiar, enduring "packaging." Their unique synthesis of repurposing preexistent mythologies while myth-making in new and creative ways is integral to both understanding their works in a holistic way (plot, structure, themes, characters, motivations) and in a particular sense (depictions of the environment and their significance).

Myth-Making and Sacred Nature also compares Tolkien's Roman Catholic perspective with Herbert's Zen Buddhist frame of reference. These two different perspectives inform their fiction in unique ways, and thus offer specific contrasts that deepen and enrich how we can understand these works. For example, Tolkien's model of environmental stewardship draws obvious parallels with Judeo-Christian hierarchical values and responsibilities. Herbert, however, while also suggesting environmental care can stem from stewardship, subverts traditional patterns of Christian thought, instead offering a Zen Buddhist interpretation of the paradox set up by predestination on the one side and unpredictable chaos on the other. These contrasting perspectives are similarly valuable in understanding our current ecological crises, as they offer readers inspiration from the environmental care suggested by Tolkien's and Herbert's moral and spiritual belief systems and reflected in their mythopoeic fantasy. In a society that increasingly devalues the environment by putting strains on our natural resources and embracing consumerism at nearly all cost, my hope is that readers will find both enrichment in the careful scrutiny of these works *and* respond to the pressing need for this ecocritical analysis.

Chapter 1 lays out definitions of mythopoeia, especially Tolkien's three functions of fantasy: recovery, a new perspective gained by reading a fantasy story; escape, a reminder to the reader of his or her longing for a better world, which fantasy can depict; and consolation, the ability of a fantasy story to renew a reader's feelings of hope, faith, joy, and even to stir an appreciation of beauty and the transcendent. Recovery, escape, and consolation in these particular books are intrinsically connected to the authors' ecocritical messages and offer consequential interpretations regardless of a reader's religious or moral persuasion. This chapter also lays out some basic ecocritical principles drawn from various positions, as well as argues for a vision of how Tolkien's and Herbert's mythopoeic fantasies present nature as numinous—that is, nature takes on a quasi-religious quality that characters encounter as wondrous and that can inspire readers to reenvision their own natural world as divine.

Chapters 2 and 3 offer examples of how each author has described the environment, how different environments function, how characters relate to their environments, and what these three things reveal. In addition, I draw upon recent research surrounding these works, particularly those scholars examining ecocritical, ethical, and spiritual issues. In doing so, I explain and define the different ecological models presented in Middle-earth and Arrakis (the desert planet of *Dune*). These models include agrarianism, conservationism, preservation, horticulture, neglect or abuse of nature, and others. Each model is significant in terms of its implications for the fictional characters and locations, as well as for the writers' own perspectives and, of course, for their readers; while these chapters cannot deal with all models comprehensively, they assert patterns of healthful and harmful environmental relationships that inform readers' understandings of the authors' attitudes toward nature.

Chapter 4 explores the role that language plays in reinforcing the authors' environmental themes and the aforementioned patterns of healthy/unhealthy environmental care; both Tolkien and Herbert had avid interests in and adeptness with language, and their invented languages and use of environmental language ("ecological semantics") further support nature as a significant and inextricable part of their world-building. In particular, Tolkien utilizes invented names of characters, races, and locations to reveal inherent connections between that which is named and the natural world. However, Herbert utilizes environmental language both structurally (following the rhythms of nature and even emulating principles of chaos theory) and dialectically, as interior monologues and dialogue between characters expose significant semantic meanings and engage readers in unique ways, yet always supporting the ecological themes at work in his writings.

Finally, chapter 5 presents a combination of biographical details and textual passages to explore some of the authors' life experiences that perhaps come to bear on their ecological and spiritual values. This chapter offers insight into the interconnectedness between lived experience and ideology, though it also moves beyond particular spiritual interpretations to establish the universal meaning and application of a mythopoeic framework. This meaning is especially significant as it relates to issues of the environment, which impact each of us, regardless of religious, political, or social persuasions.

There is an ever-growing body of academic criticism surrounding both Tolkien and Herbert, especially in light of recent film and television adaptations, suggesting there is an interest in this research and an audience for it.

By putting these texts in conversation with one another, I address a "gap" in research, since these authors have not really been analyzed side by side, nor with this particular analytical lens. This ecocritical lens adds a new dimension to how we see these works, both in their particular historical context and what they offer contemporary audiences. While Tolkien and Herbert were undoubtedly shaped by social and cultural forces of their times, their literature has in common an imperative message: that a healthy, satisfying existence is only possible with a profound and selfless appreciation and preservation of nature. While this appreciation or preservation can take multiple forms (as we will see in their fantasies), these two authors as a whole advocate for a more comprehensive vision of human-nonhuman relationships. Thus, I see *Myth-Making and Sacred Nature* as significant in at least two ways: it synthesizes existing knowledge and research about these authors while applying a unique analytical framework, thus filling the abovementioned "gap" and offering sustained, specific comparisons between the works; and it demonstrates the continuing relevancy of these authors' common theme of environmental value and stewardship, and that theme's implications for us, their readers.

CHAPTER 1

MIRRORS AND THE NUMINOUS

Mythopoeia, Ecocriticism, and Sacred Nature

Few readers would deny the ambitious scope and impact of Tolkien's and Herbert's fantastic fiction. These works have an amount of detail in their world-building that make them epic in scale, with readers often drawing comparisons between the Legendarium and the Duniverse (as *The Lord of the Rings* and the six *Dune* novels are often referred to, respectively). As Arthur C. Clarke famously said of *Dune,* "I know nothing comparable to it except [*The*] *Lord of the Rings.*"[1] The commercial success of these works leaves little doubt as to their enduring impact: each of the six *Dune* novels has sold several million copies, while Tolkien's trilogy alone has sold over 100 million copies. What makes these works so enduring? Their entertainment value, certainly: good writing, exciting plots, and memorable characters. But is there perhaps something *more* that has generations of readers and viewers, if one includes film and television adaptations of these works, returning to these stories? By examining claims from scholars such as Marek Oziewicz, Ursula K. Le Guin, Greg Garrard, Timothy Clark, Patrick Curry, Chris Brawley, and Tolkien himself, this chapter will explore the definitions of mythopoeic fantasy and ecocriticism, positing that the Legendarium and Duniverse present readers with subversive mythologies that challenge our relationship with the environment by accenting the numinous potential of nature, both within these imagined worlds and our real ecosystems. This numinous environmental focus is a reason, though not the only one, why these works proliferate the genre and literary fiction markets and continue to entertain, delight, and inspire readers. The characteristics of mythopoeia, ecocriticism, and the numinous detailed below provide an analytical framework that will be necessary for subsequent chapters; through this framework, readers can more clearly understand Tolkien's and Herbert's moral visions for a more unified relationship between humanity and the natural world, a relationship still vital for readers today.

Mythopoeic Fantasy: A Definition

In Tolkien's seminal 1947 article "On Fairy-Stories," the author offers an interpretation of mythopoeia that has become foundational to fantasy studies. Tolkien begins by tracing the difference between "childish" fairy tales and those comprising the kind of fantasy Tolkien valued:[2] "A 'fairy-story' is one which touches on or uses Faërie, whatever its own main purpose may be: satire, adventure, morality, fantasy. Faërie itself may perhaps most nearly be translated by Magic—but it is magic of a peculiar mood and power, at the furthest pole from the vulgar devices of the laborious, scientific, magician."[3] In essence, this might be one of the first major "defenses" of speculative fiction. As Tolkien acknowledges early in his article, fantasy takes various forms and is a difficult genre to define; it is something similar to "Magic" that is perhaps felt—a "peculiar mood," "a quality of strangeness and wonder"[4]—rather than categorized. Indeed, Tolkien acknowledges that fantasy's "essential drawback" is how challenging it can be to "achieve" such a mood.[5] Yet, its indefinable nature allows for exciting flexibility in what qualifies as fantastic, such as how this genre makes space for the *Dune* chronicles and other "science fantasy" or crossover works, blurring genre distinctions; in short, the individual qualities belonging to science fiction, fantasy, and other genres become less important than their cumulative effect on readers. The feeling evoked by a story is often more than the sum of its individual parts: "It is precisely the colouring, the atmosphere, the unclassifiable individual details of a story, and above all the general purport that informs with life the undissected bones of the plot, that really count."[6] Thus, one of the first parallels readers can draw between the Legendarium and the Duniverse is the cumulative effect they both achieve through fantasy and mythopoeia. By way of their extensive world-building and myth-making (essential aspects of mythopoeia), these authors provide an immersive experience, transporting readers into the "mood" and "atmosphere" of a fantastic story.[7]

Despite fantastic fiction's blurry boundaries, Tolkien makes a compelling argument for its actual usefulness throughout "On Fairy-Stories" by classifying and expounding on the various functions fantasy has for readers, including recovery, escape, and consolation, which will be defined below. By providing these categories, Tolkien offers readers and critics a valuable tool for assessing whether a mythopoeic fantasist has created not just a believable world but also a believable humanity (whatever form that "humanity" might take, as will be seen in later chapters), complete with its own philosophical worldviews and ethical complexities. In this sense, both Tolkien and Herbert imagine worlds that are not only realistically detailed geographically, linguistically, and culturally but that arguably put forth—whether overtly or implicitly—a concern for the natural world and its inhabitants, setting a unique and significant precedent for later works of fantastic fiction.[8] These works achieve a feeling of familiarity and timelessness because of their mythopoeic qualities as they draw upon prior myths and archetypes, yet they also provide a timely relevance for contemporary readers by way of their subversive reenvisioning of nature.

From Tolkien's article, later speculative fiction scholars have established their own definitions for mythopoeic fantasy, of which Oziewicz's 2008 study of mythopoeic texts offers a demarcation: "Mythopoeic fantasy is a story which provides an imaginative experience of a world in which metaphysical concepts are objective realities and the protagonists' responses to those realities reflect on their lives."[9] I would add that "the protagonists' response" has the potential to reflect on readers' lives as well, both enhancing their "imaginative experience" as they read these stories and contributing to the story's potential for real-world impact in their lives. Oziewicz also explains that a mythopoeic text differentiates itself from other kinds of speculative fiction by drawing from myths and archetypes to lend credibility and realism to the characters' psychological motivations and behaviors. The goal of such mythic inspiration is "to 'support serious consideration of religious and psychological questions.'"[10] Mythopoeic works push these "serious" questions to the forefront of the characters' and our own consciousness for pivotal reasons: "Since for most mythopoeic fantasists our humanness is to a great extent constituted by the recognition of the ethical dimension of existence, mythopoeic fantasy is a story about the protagonists' struggle to meet specific moral imperatives in the secondary world; the story which suggests why similar imperatives in the Primary World demand certain kinds of behavior."[11] Such distinction between Primary and Secondary worlds is significant. According to Tolkien and Oziewicz, there is a difference between a willing suspension of disbelief (as we often do with a particularly absurd adventure movie, for example) and what Tolkien dubs "Secondary Belief."

To achieve Secondary Belief in readers, Tolkien maintains that the mythopoeic writer takes on the responsibility of a "sub-creator." Instead of inventing a "fictional" world in the sense of "falseness," he or she builds a visionary version of reality: "Inside [the Secondary World], what he relates is 'true': it accords with the laws of that world. You therefore believe it, while you are, as it were, inside. The moment disbelief arises, the spell is broken; the magic, or rather art, has failed. You are then out in the Primary World again, looking at the little abortive Secondary World from outside."[12] Here, Tolkien describes effective writing (the "magic" and "art" of a well-crafted story), but he also asserts that the Secondary World evokes trust and belief in this world (thus, Secondary Belief) and therefore has the power to influence our view of the Primary World. If done successfully, we achieve recovery; if done poorly, we merely have a "little abortive" fiction. The imaginary worlds mythopoeic fantasists create are no less effective because they do not take place in the real world of "serious" literature. Instead, in Tolkien's words, "Fantasy . . . is, I think, not a lower but a higher form of Art, indeed the most nearly pure form, and so (when achieved) the most potent."[13] Because of its ability to "enchant" readers via its use of Faërie, an otherworldly mood, and because of recovery, escape, and consolation, mythopoeic fantasy has a unique power to shape and reshape audience's conceptions of reality.

Oziewicz's earlier assertions regarding "the ethical dimension of existence" and characters' "moral imperatives" solidify the kinds of territory mythopoeic fantasy texts cover. In such an effort, mythopoeic fantasists typically craft plots of "dire danger on the global, universal, cosmic scale into which the protagonist gets involved through a concatenation of events."[14] While these events may at first appear inconsequential, our protagonists soon face "ultimately monumental issues. They almost always feel overwhelmed by what they are expected to do."[15] The characters are allowed the freedom to make autonomous decisions, which "extends to making mistakes, sometimes serious ones."[16] The qualities of being "overwhelmed" and "making mistakes" humanize these characters, offering opportunities for emotional resonance with readers that support the larger purpose of mythopoeic fantasy, to encourage consideration of an audience's own moral perspectives. Traditional mythologies do not typically allow for the same emotional connections between character and reader; mythic protagonists can be "flat"; mythopoeic protagonists are allowed the freedom to think, act, and even fail. As a result, these characters can mirror readers' own experiences in realistic and compelling ways.

Ultimately, these mythopoeic texts lead from Bildungsroman-esque tropes into something of a profounder nature, raising questions of ethical behavior by framing the protagonists' choices in the face of physical, psychological, and sometimes even spiritual tests. Oziewicz reveals what insight readers gain from seeing these choices play out:

> Thus the plot of mythopoeic fantasy is poised between two extreme positions: pessimistic-materialistic as human beings on their own in a hostile, godless world of chance, and arrogant-religious as human beings who are instruments of a higher power which will see them through to the realization of Its objectives. Mythopoeic fantasy stresses personal responsibility and the need for concerted action in the world equally as it does the need for trust in the existence of a higher power to which all beings are tied and which steers the universe with all its creatures to the ultimate fulfillment of their destiny.[17]

Readers can be impacted by a sense of "personal responsibility" when they see a three-dimensional, emotive character faced with complex ethical dilemmas. Moreover, readers could even be prompted to consider their own "need for trust in the existence of a higher power to which all beings are tied." To be clear, mythopoeic fantasy does not require a particular dogmatic religious conviction on the part of either the characters or the readers, though Oziewicz employs language that suggests the possibility of such a requirement; instead, these texts provoke consideration of unifying forces of different kinds, the ways in "which all beings are tied" to each other, and, in many cases, the ways we are tied to our environments. Indeed, as we will see, the language Oziewicz uses above can also be interpreted as ecocritical, an analytical perspective typically separated from organized religious doctrines.

To see how mythopoeic texts might prompt such considerations of "personal responsibility and the need for concerted action," we can turn to Tolkien's functions of fantasy, the first of which is recovery. By placing readers within an imagined Secondary World (Middle-earth, for example, or Arrakis), the mythopoeic fantasist offers a new, at times even radical, perspective of place, people, and values, one that (if well-written and engaging enough) can stir the reader to bring this new gaze back to the Primary World to renew or *recover* the beauty and value inherent in that world. In Tolkien's opinion, "We should look at green again, and be startled anew (but not blinded) by blue and yellow and red. We should meet the centaur and the dragon, and then perhaps suddenly behold, like the ancient shepherds, sheep, and dogs, and horses—and wolves. This recovery fairy-stories help us to make."[18] A well-used and fitting example of "startling" recovery from Tolkien's own Legendarium are the Ents; Tolkien joins the familiar (trees) with the novel (walking, talking, feeling trees) to evoke an emotional connection between the Ents and readers.[19] After "traveling" with Treebeard in *The Two Towers,* many readers would be hard-pressed to see trees in their own back yards or at the local park in the same way as before (if, indeed, that indifference was their prior attitude)—as merely lifeless objects to be used or destroyed for human convenience.[20]

Chris Brawley reflects on how recovery and subcreation combine to reorder readers' perceptions and shift attitudes toward nature:

> According to Tolkien, this is the function of the sub-creator, an artist who is imitating God's original creative act. Sub-creation requires an act of subversion, a reordering of normal modes of perception. The result of this reordering, which Tolkien terms "Enchantment," invites the reader to a religious view of the world. So the question must now be asked: what is the value in this literary subversion? Merely to entertain? To help us escape the world around us? On the contrary, at the center of this activity is the more self-aware engagement in the "real" world through which comes a rediscovery or a "recovery" of its divine nature.[21]

Herbert, too, utilizes subversion as a means of "self-aware engagement" with the Primary World's "divine nature"[22] when he highlights resource conservation in *Dune*; by placing the novel's actions on a desert planet, Herbert frames the value of water in a new light: water is a "precious mystery." Seen in the Primary World as rude, even insulting behavior, spitting becomes a "gift [of the] body's moisture."[23] As a result of this reenvisioning, readers might be moved to see water in this light, as well. For, as Tolkien asserts, "Recovery . . . is a re-gaining—regaining of a clear view. I do not say 'seeing things as they are' and involve myself with the philosophers, though I might venture to say 'seeing things as we are (or were) meant to see them'—as things apart from ourselves."[24] "Regaining a clear view" of "things as we are meant to see them" is perhaps the most important quality of recovery, a quality that fortifies mythopoeic fantasy readers' ethical considerations. Implicit in Tolkien's assertions is the notion that mythopoeic fantasy can show readers a *better* way in the Secondary World and, by extension, suggest the possibility for a *better* reality in the Primary World. Isolating this "revision" in an entirely new or fanciful context allows our scrutiny to be sharply focused on "things apart from ourselves," but fortunately, we return to the Primary World with a new tool that, should we choose to use it, can help guide our opinions, attitudes, and behaviors in positive ways.

Fantasy writer Ursula K. Le Guin echoes these ideas in her consideration of science fiction (a term Le Guin interchanges with fantasy and whose ideas resonate with the aims of mythopoeic fantasy texts). Responding to familiar criticisms leveled at science fiction and, indeed, genre literature—that it is written for children, that it is poorly written, that it is "represented not as a means of understanding, a mirror of the real"[25]—Le Guin adopts a position in line with Tolkien's "On Fairy-Stories." For her, the merits of science fiction are the merits of all literature and art, to reveal truth:

> Writers write for their own time, for living readers. They wish to communicate the way they see life. The strange devices and metaphors used by science-fiction writers—the spaceships faster than light, the weird worlds and alien beings, the intolerable or utopian societies, the dooms envisaged, the glories imagined—all these may be entertaining toys for the fancy, but they may also be ways of seeing reality now. They are the medium used by certain serious artists to describe what all artists try to describe: this world, ourselves, the way we go.[26]

Fantasy, too, employs "strange devices and metaphors": wands and cauldrons, enchantment and wizards, greedy dragons and courageous knights; fantasy, too, employs these tropes as "ways of seeing reality now," of encouraging us to see "ourselves" in that which is strange, new, or even disquieting. Whether the work uses futuristic technology yet to be invented or looks to an imagined, mythic past, mythopoeic texts are at their most impactful when appealing to "living readers"; when "the mirror [of fantasy] seems to distort, to give a fantastic image . . . because the reality seen by the artist strikes him as distorted, as incredible";[27] and when this "mirror" explores and subverts our notions of ethical systems, healthful relationships with our environment, and humanity's potential for positive change. This study argues Tolkien's Legendarium and Herbert's Duniverse show readers both how things are—political corruption, natural resource depletion, and rampant consumerism without serious assessment of their consequences, to name a few examples—and yet also how things could be. The wide array of flawed human and nonhuman characters in these works reflect back to us our own human corruptibility, while the protagonists provide a "clear view" of how we can and should make more ethical, productive decisions, even on an individual and mundane scale (see in particular chapter 3's treatment of the Hobbits and the Atreides).

The benefit for readers in participating in fantasy's recovery can operate on a personal level as well. Tolkien writes of how we can rediscover the pleasure of what has become mundane through familiarity: "We say we know them [familiar things]. They have become like the things which once attracted us by their glitter, or their colour, or their shape, and we laid hands on them, and then locked them in our hoard, acquired them, and acquiring ceased to look at them."[28] Like Smaug in *The Hobbit,* we hoard what could be new, precious, and useful to us but that has instead fallen into disuse. This passage raises pertinent questions for the contemporary reader: How has our modern age numbed us to the charms of what we have, including nature? How has acquisition lessened the power and impact of what should be "attractive"? Is this the fate of all ownership—that is, by owning a thing, it loses its appeal for the owner? Mythopoeic fantasy offers some answers to these questions: "mythopoeic fantasy seeks to provide readers with 'a new vision . . . of ordinary reality [that] restores our own world to us' but is enriched with 'an emotional experience of harmony and reunification.'"[29] When we "behold" anew (to borrow Tolkien's language) the "glitter," "color," and "shape" of familiar objects, we are taking the first steps toward "harmony and reunification"; Tolkien and Herbert support these steps by way of their imaginative depictions of new worlds and laudable protagonists.

Tolkien's next function of fantasy, escape, requires fantastic recovery first to be most effective. If recovery suggests that something needs to be reenvisioned (that is, we have lost our true "vision of reality"), then escape offers the vision itself, or at least *a* vision, via the Secondary World. By way of imaginative creatures, new worlds, and other fantasy "tropes," readers can find pleasure and rest in such an escape. Tolkien defends the idea of a real need for "escapist" literature, asserting that the "escape of the prisoner" is too often confused with the "flight of the deserter."[30] In essence, the first implies that the prisoner desires and needs the escape, actively seeking a way out from his circumstances for legitimate reasons. However, the flight of the deserter is a turning away from, a leaving behind, or a giving up on. Tolkien contrasts the bravery and cowardice of the two actions. Demands from the Primary World are often overwhelming, producing a profound "desire to escape, not indeed from life, but from our present time and self-made misery."[31] Tolkien adds to the list of miseries: "hunger, thirst, poverty, pain, sorrow, injustice, death."[32] Fantasy offers a space for readers to turn aside from these pains, to escape in the best sense of the word. The restful fields and hills of the Shire, idyllically tucked away in Middle-earth, or the stunningly vast and open desert of Arrakis with its mystical indigenous customs, give readers an engrossing entry into a refreshingly different time and space. Thus, we might describe escape as a unique reading experience resulting from a well-imagined, well-crafted story that takes place in a convincing Secondary World and contributes to the reader's emotional restoration.

Restoration from escape leads directly into fantasy's third function, consolation. While readers escape into a Secondary World and are caught up in its events and characters, the plot moves toward a resolution, which Tolkien claims has the potential to be mythopoeic fantasy's "highest function,"[33] a simultaneously painful and joyful turn of events leading to a "happy ending" or *eucatastrophe*: "In such stories when the sudden 'turn' comes we get a piercing glimpse of joy, and heart's desire, that for a moment passes outside the frame, rends indeed the very web of the story, and lets a gleam come through."[34] If a conventional story, fantasy or otherwise, offers a satisfying conclusion because all loose ends are "tied up," a mythopoeic fantasy offers instead a more profound and thought-provoking ending, touching on a deep human "desire" for hope, joy, and the consolation of what our lives *could* be. (In this study, I will later focus on how the Legendarium and the Duniverse portray nature in a sacramental light and what hope this sacramental vision offers readers. Other "joyous turns" can of course be found in these works besides the sacralization of nature.)

Tolkien's and Herbert's Secondary worlds offer readers the imaginative scope to find newfound hope and healing via recovery, escape, and consolation; moreover, intersections between mythopoeia, ecocriticism, and spirituality are some of the spaces we can look for this hope and healing. Tolkien famously observed, "Even fairy-stories as a whole have three faces: the Mystical towards the supernatural; the Magical towards Nature; and the Mirror of scorn and pity towards Man. The essential face of Faërie is the middle one, the Magical."[35] As Patrick Curry analyzes, specific parts of the Legendarium correspond to each of these three "faces," which Curry names as the spiritual, the natural, and the social. He ascribes a geographical "domain" to each of these categories: "the Sea," "Middle-earth," and "the Shire."[36] Applying this model to Herbert's mythopoeic fantasy can show how the Duniverse has these faces, as well.[37] In essence, the "human" beings[38] in the Duniverse are "Man," belonging to the social domain. "Nature" extends to several natural spaces, though most prominently the Arrakeen desert; finally, the merging of Leto II with the sandworms, begun in *Children of Dune* and thus enacting the Atreides' ultimate ecological plan, is one of the "Mystical" faces. Indeed, Curry contends that analyzing the domains reveals both environmental and spiritual dimensions to Tolkien's Secondary worlds: "Rising above the dogmas of his own religious upbringing, Tolkien has thus made it possible for his readers to unselfconsciously combine Christian ethics and a neo-pagan reverence for nature, together with (no less important) a liberal humanist respect for the small, precarious, and apparently mundane."[39] The same can be said of Herbert's mythopoeic fantasy. He combines Eastern religious ethics with a neopagan, indigenous "reverence for nature" and an unmistakable "liberal humanist" perspective. Ecocritical principles can shed light on how these faces interact and why considerations of nature within these mythopoeic texts are significant.

Ecocriticism

How does an ecocritical reading of *The Lord of the Rings* and the *Dune* chronicles together intersect with the mythopoeic qualities detailed above? Moreover, how does such an ecocritical analysis benefit readers? Mythopoeic texts can move readers toward a fuller and more harmonious, unified vision (how things are meant to be, or at least how they *might* be) of human and environmental relationships. In essence, this movement is also at the heart of ecocriticism, which examines how various fields, including and especially literature, portray issues of human connection and disconnection with the natural world, and to what degree literature addresses or contributes to harmful attitudes toward our ecosystems. A unique attribute of this form of literary criticism is its real-world focus; ecocritics are concerned not just with how literature portrays ideology, but how ideology can be applied to our lived experiences, especially individual, collective, and governmental responsibility:

Ecocriticism describes and confronts the socially uneven encounters and entanglements of earthly living, from petro-capitalism to cancer stories to the poetry of bird song. As a political mode of literary and cultural analysis, ecocriticism aims to understand and intervene in the destruction and diminishment of living worlds. Ranging in its critical engagements across historical periods, cultural texts, and cultural formations, ecocriticism focuses on the aesthetic modes, social meanings, contexts, genealogies, and counterpoints of cultural practices that contribute to ecological ruination and resilience. A core premise is that environmental crises have social, cultural, affective, imaginative, and material dimensions.[40]

Like mythopoeic fantasy, this field desires "serious" consideration of profoundly impactful issues because it recognizes the inherent interconnections between the environment and various other "dimensions" of human life. Ecocritical concerns also reckon with the notion of how things *should* be in opposition to what they are (akin to mythopoeic escape and recovery): "To describe something as an ecological problem is to make a normative claim about how we would wish things to be."[41] If mythopoeic texts urge a reassessment in human attitudes toward their fellow living creatures, human and nonhuman alike, and if these texts can connect readers to a more spiritual, hopeful existence and awareness of nature's inherent numinous potential, then we must focus our attention on the points of intersection between myth-making and the environment.

Oziewicz echoes these ecocritical intersections as he describes the universal and personal natures of mythopoeic stories: "Mythopoeic fantasies, I believe, are usually 'larger projects'; they are personal 'poetic' statements by identifiable authors on what makes human life worthwhile and on our place in the universe. They *mean* to suggest the answers to those big questions, and as such they are what Lewis has called 'additions to life.'"[42] Like ecocritics, mythopoeic fantasists are concerned with the relationship between "human life" and "our place in the universe," just as ecocritics assert that human culture is connected to nature and deeply influenced by it.[43] If looked at in light of ecocritical theory, mythopoeic fantasists' "personal," "poetic statements" could point readers to reconsider their relationship with the environment. Moreover, mythopoeic fantasy urges a value system not predicated on hierarchical power but instead on trust in the unity and worth of all forms of life:

> Among most important propositions that mythopoeic fantasy nourishes and promotes are the belief in the ultimate conquest of death based on a conviction about the solidarity and continuity of all life, and the affirmation of the value of life based on ideals. The first of these is usually developed in the direction of holism and organicism which recognize the deep interconnectedness at all levels of physical, psychological, and social realities. The second is . . . an assertion that human life acquires genuine value only through our choices, albeit made in an "unheroic" setting. Life is not lived, mythopoeic fantasists suggest, for the sake of it, but for achieving human fulfillment.[44]

Through these works, readers can find inspiration for ways to "value" life through "solidarity" and to "achieve human fulfillment," possibly by contributing to our environmental future in positive, productive ways. Mythopoeic fantasists emphasize environmental concerns in much the same ways that they do other profound issues, suggesting that concerns about the natural world are as serious and pressing as any other human concern: "Not only do they stress the importance of achieving personhood, building communication with others, fostering a sense of community, and striving to realize other aspects of the human dimension, but they also warn readers about the destruction of the environment and sensitize them to the fate of non-human life forms."[45] Tolkien's and Herbert's writings certainly depict environmental destruction and, by way of their characters' actions, "warn" readers of consequences. Chapters 2 and 3 contend just how intertwined morality and ecoconsciousness are—the heroic, praiseworthy characters demonstrate care and appreciation of their ecosystems, while the "villainous" characters find every opportunity to neglect and abuse their environments. For readers, an inherent question raised is whether or not they fit into these two categories (though, of course, not in a literal sense), and if so, how their individual decisions are helping or harming their own "right relations" with the natural world. In essence, mythopoeic fantasy and ecocriticism both prompt consideration of individual choices and their consequences.

Consequences are a central theme in the Legendarium and the Duniverse, and they are no less significant in the minds of ecocritics. For both the ecocritic and the mythopoeic fantasist, the choices we make as morally conscious individuals, whether great or small, have a significant impact. Timothy Clark describes the Anthropocene, our current historical epoch, in these terms, too: "[The Anthropocene] is characterized by the unprecedented fact that humanity has come to play a decisive, if still largely incalculable, role in the planet's ecology and geology, that 'Human activities have become so pervasive and profound that they rival the great forces of nature and are pushing the Earth as a whole into planetary *terra incognita*.'"[46] If mythopoeic fantasy can raise awareness of the way in which choices within the Secondary World have consequences, "recovery" could provide a better understanding of how the same holds true in the Primary World: "'Ethical fantasy underscores that human choices and actions matter, whether they are large or small, deliberate or not, and sometimes they have even worldwide consequences.'"[47] In addition to recovery, escape, too, can provide readers with a better understanding of humanity's own desires for a more healthful relationship with nature. When readers enter Middle-earth and Arrakis, they are presented with characters whose choices have long-lasting, profound effects on their fellow creatures and homes; they can emerge from these worlds either challenged or renewed by the impact of those choices.

For Tolkien, the escapist elements of fantasy should not necessarily be used for their own sake but for emotional effect, awakening desires and prompting self-reflection: "One of these [primordial human] desires is to survey the depths of space and time. Another is (as will be seen) to hold communion with other living things. A story may thus deal with the satisfaction of these desires, with or without the operation of either machine or magic, and in proportion as it succeeds it will approach the quality and have the flavour of fairy-story."[48] This passage hearkens back to Tolkien's starting point, about the indefinable nature of fantasy; other kinds of literature can have the "fairy-story" effect of awakening these desires, but mythopoeic fantasy is well suited to evoking the wish "to hold communion with other living things" because it is by nature concerned with right relations between ourselves and "our place in the universe." More sophisticated or resonant mythopoeic fantasy works model such right relations because of their writers' subcreative power, offering writer and reader a mutually satisfying experience: "Enchantment produces a Secondary World into which both designer and spectator can enter, to the satisfaction of their senses while they are inside; but in its purity it is artistic in desire and purpose. Magic [however] produces, or pretends to produce, an alteration in the Primary World. It does not matter by whom it is said to be practiced, fay or mortal, it remains distinct from the other two; it is not an art but a technique; its desire is *power* in this world, domination of things and wills."[49] In this passage, Tolkien's language calls to mind ecocritical concern. Ecocriticism has at its core an understanding that everything is connected in a pattern,[50] which calls upon us to be aware of this pattern, how we connect with our own ecosystems, how we can work to make these connections more effective, and how doing so will enrich our own existences. Likewise, "enchantment" (the result of successful mythopoeia) has an effect that gratifies reader and writer because of its imaginative, creative power. Magic (the result of an unsuccessful sub-creation) assumes a hierarchical superiority—concerned more with "power" and "domination" than with mutual satisfaction. Therefore, the successful sub-creator does not manipulate its readers via "magic" but rather takes them deeper into reality in order to uncover truths about human experiences, desires, and concerns. As Tolkien claims, "Uncorrupted [Enchantment] does not seek delusion, nor bewitchment and domination; it seeks shared enrichment, partners in making and delight, not slaves."[51] Here, too, his word choice is evocative of harmony and connectedness: "making" and "delight" instead of "delusion" and "domination." Thus, we can say that mythopoeic fantasists and ecocritics have many of the same broad concerns and motivations: how language and literature can engage readers to reflect upon interpersonal and environmental relationships and, by this reflection, find solutions for harmony, creativity, and delight.[52] I will now turn to how mythopoeic fantasy that portrays environmental concerns presents readers with a sacralized vision of nature, placing it beyond the realm of a fictional setting to an active participant in our literary and real lives.

Nature as Numinous

Considering the above definitions of mythopoeia and ecocriticism, the question is now how mythopoeic fantasy portrays nature and what that portrayal implies for readers. In essence, mythopoeic fantasy is in a unique position to subvert traditional notions of the environment. These notions are generally based on either a hierarchical conception of humanity as superior to nature and therefore in a position to use or destroy it as needed; or on an artificial divide between humanity and nature reinforced by our sense of being separate and different from it; or both.[53] Ecoconscious subversion occurs in fantasy by replacing the image of nature as a passive, powerless object with a sacralized view of nature as a powerful, divine force with transcendent value. The effect of such a reimagined perspective can be called numinous: "The numinous . . . [is] that quality of 'holiness' in its original meaning as that which inspires awe, a meaning devoid of our modern associations of the holy as a moral category. [Rudolf] Otto promoted the idea that this numinous consciousness was the basis of the first stirrings of the religious imagination which, at their inception, were a form of religious dread, but later evolved into more complex, rational conceptions which informed most of the major religious traditions."[54] As previously recognized, mythopoeic fantasy rarely, if ever, demands a dogmatic religious conviction to be spiritually impactful. Because mythopoeia is a form of "myth-making," drawing upon preexistent myths and archetypes to create new mythologies, these stories will inevitably "repurpose" certain themes, symbols, and imagery that have come to be associated with religion; however, mythopoeic fantasists rarely do so for the overt purpose of "converting" readers to a religious belief system. Otherwise, the result would probably be akin to allegories, morality tales, or fables (which Tolkien classifies in "On Fairy-Stories" as *not* mythopoeic fantasy).

Both Tolkien and Herbert are writers whose moral perspectives can be recognized and appreciated in the context of and apart from their individual religious beliefs. Like fantasy itself, these moral perspectives are often "felt" within the mythopoeic stories rather than proscribed. Brawley describes a similar occurrence when defining the "numinous": "Otto argues that the experience of the numinous is non-rational, a religious sensibility only to be evoked or awakened rather than dogmatized."[55] Chapters 2 and 3 examine that while nature frequently becomes a setting for the numinous, evoking awe, holiness, and a spiritual connection for the protagonists and readers alike, it is rarely done under the purview of any religious authority; and if it is, such authority is called into question along with other establishments of power.[56]

Mythopoeic scholars have been careful to show the nonreligious capacity of fantasy, even when these scholars are themselves arguing that writers like Tolkien or C. S. Lewis can bring readers closer to an apprehension of the "divine." In fact, some critics see fantasy and other genre fiction as a modern replacement for religion, in the sense that these stories can offer readers an emotionally and psychologically resonant experience that conventional religion might not: "[Scholar Kath] Filmer suggests that in the modern, secular society fantasy has, to a certain extent, replaced religion. . . . 'I do not mean to propose that the authors of science fiction and fantasy texts are "putting religion into the story." . . . Rather I believe that the discourse of the fantastic is itself a form of religious discourse, with all the features of didacticism, persuasion and emotive languages which have traditionally been associated with the discourse of religion.'"[57] Tolkien's third function of fantasy, *eucatastrophe,* evokes the language of religion: "miraculous grace: never to be counted on to recur."[58] Yet, the events of the Legendarium and the Duniverse do not require a deity or "god" to intervene and save our protagonists; it is through their own efforts and sacrifices that they find "miraculous grace." Tolkien asserts that after the "piercing joy" of consolation occurs, a reader still has an individual responsibility to create joy and purpose in his or her own life: "The Christian has still to work, with mind as well as body, to suffer, hope, and die; but he may now perceive that all his bents and faculties have a purpose, which can be redeemed."[59] Within an ecocritical framework, the non-Christian, too, has a responsibility to strive for a better quality of human and environmental relations, just as the mythopoeic protagonists have modeled for readers.

While this book is focused on what the Legendarium and the Duniverse offer readers from a mythopoeic, ecocritical perspective, it by no means attempts to address or proscribe all the different enriching perspectives that can be drawn by readers from either the texts being analyzed or fantasy in general. However, mythopoeic fantasy does hold a powerful potential for reconnecting readers with a sense of existence beyond or outside of themselves:

> "Literature of revision allows people to escape from their culture's imperfect systems of authority based on reason, and lets them experience other possibilities for ordering experience, whether religious or utopian." . . . Fantasy is a veiled religious activity [which] can revise our perceptions of the natural world. . . . This literature of revision endows the reader with a sacramental vision of the world, not only as it exists in the fantasy novel, but metaphorically as a means of recreating his or her own world once the book has been put down.[60]

Here, Brawley synthesizes what Tolkien and Oziewicz have claimed in their own mythopoeic analyses—that "revision" contrasts the "imperfect systems of authority" with "other possibilities for ordering experience"; after emerging from the escape and Secondary Belief the fantasy work offers, a reader can now "recreate" in the Primary World such a "sacramental vision" that was afforded by the story in the Secondary World. And, Brawley maintains, mythopoeic fantasy's sacramental vision is consciously and specifically "attempting to recreate . . . a new mythology in order to infuse readers with the sense of the transcendent which is no longer accessible, for many people, in religion."[61] As such, mythopoeic fantasy fits between two places: the marvelous and the fantastic.[62]

Like science fiction, mythopoeic texts join two forces to create an effect in the reader. In the case of science fiction, plausible scientific theories provide support for fantastical, "unreal" events; in mythopoeic fantasy, seemingly supernatural or marvelous elements combine with the "plausible" fantasy world (again, Secondary Belief because of a well-crafted sub-creation) to create specific reactions in the reader. According to Brawley, subversion is one among those reactions:

> For these authors, their works are meant to be subversive, both in the sense of disturbing or unsettling the reader, and in the sense of engaging the imagination in the created secondary world, so that the "real" world can be transformed as the result of the re-vision initiated in the encounter with the fantasy world.... A desire to escape the world only to be comforted in a fantasy landscape is *not* at the core of the mythopoeic imagination. What concerns our authors is the desire to use fantastic elements subversively to reorganize and recombine normative modes of perception in order to revision the world in a more sacramental way.[63]

Interestingly, Brawley identifies that escape in and of itself is not mythopoeic fantasy's goal, as Tolkien also claimed. Escape into the Secondary World *can* cause distraction from our "self-made miseries" and the demands of everyday life, but the more meaningful "reorganization" and "recombination" of "normative modes of perception" can also emerge from the escape; an ecocritical reading of such works can reinforce understanding of how mythopoeic fantasists use subversive fantastic elements.

Brawley too connects his treatment of mythopoeic fantasy with ecocritical ideological principles, which at their inception "sought to offer 'an alternative view of existence that [would] provide an ethical and conceptual foundation for right relations with the earth.'"[64] However, Brawley focuses not only on how ecocriticism raises issues of environmental concern but how it also raises issues of ethical concern, which is perhaps more pertinent: "In his much debated article 'The Historical Roots of our Environmental Crisis,' Lynn White states that our attempts at proposals for environmental care are ineffective; what must be addressed is the underlying ideologies which inform the way nature is perceived. White states, 'What people do about their ecology depends on what they think about themselves in relation to things around them.'"[65] In other words, environmental solutions lack efficacy if human attitudes toward nature remain unchanged. Hierarchical views of human superiority and blamelessness juxtaposed against nature's inferiority and "otherness" are some of the perspectives that need to be shifted to promote "right relations with the earth." Ecocriticism advocates for how literature is uniquely positioned to speak to "the underlying ideologies which inform" perceptions of nature because it can engage with readers' imaginations and emotions in ways that data or "proposals for environmental care" might not. And, as Brawley will argue, mythopoeic fantasy offers specific ideological shifts addressing hierarchical, anthropocentric attitudes that interfere with a more harmonious, empathetic quality of existence.

First, however, Brawley raises the question of how religion and mythology, particularly the traditional Western beliefs embodied in them, present nature and potentially contribute to the current harmful ideologies working against environmental care. One of the first harmful beliefs is that of a dichotomy between humans, nature, and God: "In many of [mythologist Joseph Campbell's] works, he refers to Western mythology as participating in 'mythic dissociation'. . . . Since the nature of God is transcendent (somehow 'out there'), and man is to have 'dominion' over the earth, humans are dissociated from the divine; God is not in the world, in humans, or in nature. This mythic dissociation is not to be found in Eastern religions such as Buddhism, Daoism, or Hinduism. In fact, in these religions it is quite the opposite."[66] Later analysis in this study will examine how several of the communities in the Legendarium illustrate the effects of a similar "mythic dissociation." Because they have either lost sight of the "divine" in nature, or never recognized it to begin with, these communities exercise varying levels of "dominion" over their ecosystems, ranging from the outright devastating (Sauron's wastelands in and surrounding Mordor, or Saruman's rampant industrialization near Isengard) to the less obviously problematic (the Elves' "improvement" on nature, or the Dwarves' exploitation of mines for precious gems).[67] And while Herbert's Duniverse is nowhere near free from environmental misuse, the communities that are grounded in Eastern religious traditions (especially the Fremen, Bene Gesserit, and Atreides) tend to adapt to the needs of nature more readily and effectively, perhaps because of this system's lack of any apparent "mythic dissociation." This is not to say, however, that Tolkien is advocating for such dichotomies between humans and nature, nor that Herbert is ignoring these dichotomies. Instead, for mythopoeic fantasists like Tolkien, "capturing the sense of the numinous and subverting normative perceptions of the natural world is the end goal," despite their place within a "Western" worldview. Authors like Herbert (though

Brawley did not include Herbert in his study) work differently from Tolkien, but with similar "end goals" for their mythopoeic texts:

> What is noticed in this story is that the divine nature of the world is present within all creation, and the God-human-nature hierarchy is not. Campbell terms this immanent ideology "mythic association." . . . Thus [they] broaden the perspective of mythopoeic fantasists who are willing to both challenge the Western mythos and also employ other mythological traditions. . . . In contrast to Christian influenced authors such as . . . Tolkien, [these other writers] write from within a more mystical, more mythically associated worldview.[68]

Later chapters will identify more specifically the ways in which Middle-earth and Arrakis play with "mythic association/disassociation" by presenting different "mythological traditions" and the "mystical worldview" resulting from such traditions.

Brawley also considers what solutions, if any, to flawed environmental ideologies mythopoeic fantasy poses. Based on White and Campbell's critiques of Western perceptions regarding humans and nature, Brawley posits that Western religion has lost its recognition of the numinous, which leads readers to fantasy as a type of replacement-religion: "[Campbell] also realizes that the bigger problem lies in the fact that this mythological system has lost its sense of participation in the mystery of the universe. This participation in the transcendent reality which informs the world is Campbell's first function of a living mythology. . . . Thus, the problem is not with Christianity as such, but its loss of a sense of mystery."[69] His claim directly supports the aims of ecocriticism: our "participation" in environmental healing is desperately needed in order to create real change; participation of another kind, in the "mystery of the universe" and "transcendent reality" that mythopoeic fantasy enables (in the same way mythology does), is a pivotal way in which to engage readers with a sense of the religious without compelling them to adhere to a religion. It seems no surprise that both *The Lord of the Rings* and the *Dune* chronicles enjoyed great popularity in the United States and Europe in the 1970s, reaching a generation coping with enormous cultural and philosophical shifts; these works evoked a sense of entertainment and joy, but perhaps they also provided participation in an experience that was missing from their daily lives in a postmodern world that questioned the inherent value and meaning in religion, politics, and conventional social norms.

For postmodern and contemporary readers alike (if indeed such a distinction is needed), mythopoeic fantasy portrays two important concepts that when combined can contribute to ideological shifts in perceptions of the environment: animism and interrelatedness (Brawley). According to Brawley, "Animism assumes that the world all around us is alive, and that all beings have the ability to communicate (if we just listen)."[70] Animism disrupts traditional conceptions of humanity as the "center of any dialogue," an anthropocentric attitude that makes it "difficult for modern Christianity to re-envision relations with the environment."[71] Fantasy, however, "offers the reader an animistic way of perceiving the natural world," and its Secondary worlds "give us a sense of awe towards the created world, a fresh way of viewing reality anew, and a way of recovering what was lost."[72] Moreover, interrelatedness breaks down the barrier between human and nonhuman categories. Brawley sees interrelatedness as raising significant "questions" about the nature of this barrier, such as if it truly exists: "[Is] this just an abstraction, a function of language? Where does one organism stop and another begin? What exactly is the nature of the subject/object relationship? By asking such questions, our most basic cultural and religious concepts are attacked, and it allows for the possibility for new ways to engage with the world."[73] If Brawley is correct, animism and interrelatedness reveal "new ways" to think, feel, and act regarding our relationship with the environment. Furthermore, if the environment is framed as sacred, a place of reconnecting with a religious, transcendent experience missing from our daily lives, the "possibility for new ways to engage with the world" is enhanced immensely because we can begin to see nature with the same value and mystery that we often ascribe to our human relationships. We might even be led to invoke feelings of inclusivity, compassion, and empathy for our ecosystems.

In view of the definitions this chapter explored, readers can apprehend a meaningful use for mythopoeic fantasy, ecocriticism, and a sacralized view of nature. Moreover, these theories have the potential to connect readers to mythopoeic fantasists through the act of sub-creation. Author and reader enter into a profound relationship via the imaginary world and fantastical elements: by going through the steps of recovery, escape, and consolation, the reader can emerge a *different* reader—disrupted, inspired, renewed— and this is only possible because of the power of mythopoeia. The craft is not just beneficial for a detailed world and believable characters, but always there is a larger moral pattern these authors desire to convey. At the heart of this moral pattern is the existence of the divine. Mythopoeic fantasy is "a worldview which assumes the existence of the supernatural,"[74] though I would instead call this the "divine."[75] The result of such "assumptions" is a work religious and at times even mystical in feeling, partly because it draws upon "a variety of artistically recreated mythic and archetypal materials,"[76] partly because it resacralizes the very world around us. At their heart, "Fairy-stories were plainly not primarily concerned with possibility, but with desirability. If they awakened *desire,* satisfying it while often whetting it unbearably, they succeeded."[77] One of the most exciting aspects of reading mythopoeic fantasy is that it awakens desire: desire for a better existence, for more meaningful, empathetic human and environmental connections, for a renewed sense of purpose in our daily choices and their consequences. Mythopoeic fantasy can engage us through "satisfying" these desires and, truly, "whetting them unbearably" as we embark on the remarkable task of participating in these stories alongside the writers themselves: "This is Tolkien's central contention, that by producing a piece of mythopoeic fantasy, and by extension reading that piece of mythopoeic fantasy, one participates in the human engagement with creation itself. One becomes, in essence, a sub-creator."[78] If they agree with Brawley's interpretation, readers have been given the responsibility of a unique interactive role: to read, to be inspired, and to engage "with creation itself," thereby engaging with the "divine." The following chapters will analyze what that engagement looks like in Tolkien's and Herbert's sub-creative worlds.

CHAPTER 2

FORESTS AND DESERTS

Tolkien's and Herbert's Landscape Descriptions

To provide a better understanding of Tolkien's and Herbert's mythopoeic fantasy as ecocritical texts, this chapter will focus on how these two authors describe their Secondary worlds' physical landscapes, as well as how these descriptions reveal the authors' inherent attitudes toward nature. The carefully expressed details these authors use not only contribute to readers' "Secondary Belief" and make more richly specific settings for the stories' plots; they also frame natural spaces in such a way as to focus readers' attention on these spaces as new, "recoverable" visions of their own natural worlds. Moreover, by describing these places as numinous, thus giving them quasi-religious qualities, the authors demonstrate that nature offers their characters and readers a potentially transcendent experience, lending inherent personal and spiritual value to nature.

First, guiding this section's interpretation will be the recognition that nature exists in the Primary World and, as such, has real, objective consequences on the quality of readers' current and future existence. Therefore, this analysis will explore nature as more than simply an academic concept; unlike many other literary criticism theories, ecocriticism has the unique potential to join the academic and the real world: "The challenge for ecocritics is to keep one eye on the ways in which 'nature' is always in some ways culturally constructed, and the other on the fact that nature really exists, both the object and, albeit distantly, the origin of our discourse."[1] In entering these Secondary worlds, this section will attempt to stay mindful of the reality these stories should be pointing readers toward (nature affects and can be affected by us), as well as the joy and beauty these descriptions evoke for readers. Additionally, this chapter will utilize several basic ecocritical principles as part of how it analyzes the various landscape descriptions. First, "Ecocriticism undertakes rhetorical readings of environmental discourses" and "uses literary critical methods, typically close analysis of small examples";[2] the "close analysis" Garrard describes is this chapter's specific focus. While not an exhaustive catalog of every physical description in the Legendarium and Duniverse, the pages below explore patterns—patterns in how Tolkien and Herbert characterize landscapes, grouped according to loose criteria of nature as either beautiful, hybridized/anthropomorphized, regal, or abused (sometimes, these criteria overlap). Second, ecocritics adopt different "positions," each of which Garrard acknowledges affords an understanding of the global "environmental crisis in its own way, emphasizing aspects that are amenable to solutions in terms that it supplies or threatening to values it holds dear. Each one, moreover, might provide the basis for a distinct ecocritical approach with specific literary or cultural affinities and aversions."[3] These positions provide opportunities for their application to various ideas outside of nature, ideas such as growth and energy; sustainability; abuse of nature, resources, and energy; and balance/imbalance.[4] Both authors' mythopoeic fantasies explore many of these concepts, especially Herbert's writings, and chapters 4 and 5 examine closely these terms and their implications for readers.

Third, ecocritics "give special canonical emphasis to writers who foreground nature as a major part of their subject matter"[5] (to which I would add Tolkien and Herbert as representative of the speculative fiction ecocritical canon),[6] and recognize the usefulness of the narrative form as a powerful space to "be comprehensive in the way that, say, a paper in a scientific or social science journal never could be; for it is free to trace all imaginable scenarios and to survey how prejudice, personal background, cultural assumptions, scientific research and the complacencies of day-to-day life *all* form part of how people engage or evade environmental questions."[7] And because of its "comprehensive" nature, narrative works provide a powerful means of ecocritical involvement: "The stronger our sense of immersion in a narrative, of human empathy with the action and characters, then the more likely it is to enhance our understanding of how others think."[8] Finally, ecocritics reject an overly narrow focus on the "linguistic and social constructedness of the external world" that some literary theories stress; instead, they give attention to "ecocentric values of . . . collective ethical responsibility, and the claims of the world beyond ourselves."[9] This study refers repeatedly to these final ideas of "collective ethical responsibility" and "the claims of the world beyond ourselves," and I argue that Tolkien and Herbert saw ethical responsibility and the needs of the real world as pivotal parts of their fictional worlds and their own realities. The next chapter also investigates how the ways in which different communities and individual characters interact with their environments suggest to readers models of healthful and harmful environmental relationships, as well as reinforce moral worldviews such as collective ethical responsibility that readers can consider or even adopt. In both this and the next chapter, I rely on Matthew T. Dickerson and Jonathan Evans's *Ents, Elves, and Eriador* and Susan Jeffers's *Arda Inhabited* for their discussion of environmental/ethical models within the Legendarium and apply several of those models to the Duniverse. While my focus below is on slightly different effects than these authors' analyses, Dickerson and Evans's categories of stewardship and agricultural/horticultural care and Jeffers's categories of power with/from/over have been essential to drawing more sustained ecocritical comparisons between Tolkien's and Herbert's mythopoeic fantasy works.

The Shire and Arrakis: Impressionistic Nature

Throughout *The Fellowship of the Ring*'s and *Dune*'s early chapters, Tolkien and Herbert give readers brief images of the Shire and Dune, much like Impressionist painters—the effect is that of a mood or feeling. Readers become immersed in these places through many descriptive "moments," often filtered through the characters' experiences of nature. For example, the Shire is the first landscape introduced to readers in *The Lord of the Rings*. As one of the three "faces" of fantasy, this domain is the "social, cultural and political world."[10] In Curry's summation, "[The Shire] includes such things as the hobbits' strong sense of community, their decentralized parish or municipal democracy, their bioregionalism (living within an area defined by its natural characteristics, and within its limits), and their enduring love of, and feeling for, place. In all these respects, the ultimate contrast is with the brutal universalism and centralized efficiency of totalitarian Mordor."[11] Through *The Fellowship of the Ring*'s opening chapters, readers see how "community," "decentralized" government, and "bioregionalism" combine to give the Shire a feeling of casual, rustic comfort that supports the Hobbits' close relationship to their land;[12] readers can also see how the Shire is important as both plot setting and as its own force. (*Dune,* too, fits much of Curry's description—the Fremen have a strong feeling of community, put government in the hands of tribal leaders, and thrive in their particular place, the desert.[13]) The Shire provides the background for the beginning of two significant journeys—Bilbo's quest with the Dwarves to the Lonely Mountain detailed in *The Hobbit,* and Frodo's journey to Mount Doom to destroy the One Ring—but its impact and value extend beyond such backgrounding. As Curry has famously said of Middle-earth as a whole, the Shire itself is like a character:[14] living, dynamic, simultaneously symbolic in the sense that it can stand for figurative concepts, and literal because it is also a beautiful, desirable place itself, stripped of symbolism.[15]

Clearly, the Hobbits recognize the Shire's beauty and desirability; Tolkien writes that they immediately felt an emotional connection to the environment: "At once the Western Hobbits fell in love with their new land, and they remained there, and soon passed once more out of the history of Men and of Elves."[16] Following their initial crossing of the Brandywine River into what becomes known as the Shire, these Hobbits find a landscape ideally suited to their agricultural lifestyle: "The land was rich and kindly, and though it had long been deserted when they entered it, it had before been well tilled, and there the king had once had many farms, cornlands, vineyards, and woods."[17] Evidently, the Shire is a distinctive landscape, one suited to growing things; other places, such as the Old Forest or Lothlórien, exhibit their own unique qualities, some uncultivated and others ethereal. But what is more significant, as *The Silmarillion* illustrates so powerfully, Middle-earth has its own lengthy history that exists and persists despite the quarrels and achievements of Hobbits, Men, Elves, and Wizards; it existed long before these communities arrived, and the text suggests it will continue on without them, as even the above passage implies.[18] The land's "independence," as it were, underscores how nature endures as its own force and not as merely a passive object for Hobbits and other beings to manipulate. Nevertheless, the Hobbits appreciate their new land and attempt to coincide with nature.

The Hobbits' homes, too, complement the land and illustrate their coexistence with nature. Their habitations are organically shaped, either literally fitted to the land (as in the case of Hobbit holes like Bag End) or mimicking natural features (the low-storied, rustic houses bordering the Shire).[19] Daily existence in these homes is humble, but Tolkien's descriptions invite readers to see this existence as worthwhile and even perhaps idyllic. The very scenes setting up *The Fellowship of the Ring*'s grand adventure begin in an ordinary way, yet the author highlights the value in its ordinariness: "Inside Bag End, Bilbo and Gandalf were sitting at the open window of a small room looking out west on to the garden. The late afternoon was bright and peaceful. The flowers glowed red and golden: snap-dragons and sunflowers, and nasturtians [*sic*] trailing all over the turf walls and peeping in at the round windows. 'How bright your garden looks!' said Gandalf. 'Yes,' said Bilbo. 'I am very fond indeed of it, and of all the dear old Shire; but I think I need a holiday.'"[20] Tolkien's imagery paints a picture of colors and impressions: the "afternoon" light, "bright" reds and golds, a "peaceful" mood, and admiration from both Gandalf and Bilbo (notwithstanding Bilbo's decision to leave Hobbiton). Through these small yet engaging details, Tolkien allows readers to feel transported into this scene, as if sitting beside the two characters and appreciating that moment of peace and simple, homey comforts. Such moments also offer readers an entry point for fantastic recovery; by portraying an afternoon at Bag End as so cherished and inviting, Tolkien's text invites a reenvisioning of readers' own relationships to their homes, gardens, and other natural spaces.

Tolkien continues using impressionistic imagery to depict the Shire. After Bilbo's birthday party, Gandalf convinces him to leave the One Ring behind before journeying to the Elves and the mountains. In these passages, Tolkien employs nighttime descriptions to show another view of Hobbiton's natural beauty. Within a few lines, Tolkien moves the plot forward while also describing Hobbiton in such a way as to bring readers into the scene: "It was a fine night, and the black sky was dotted with stars. [Bilbo] looked up, sniffing the air. . . . He paused, silent for a moment . . . went round into his garden, and trotted down the long sloping path. He jumped over a low place in the hedge at the bottom, and took to the meadows, passing into the night like a rustle of wind in the grass."[21] Bilbo's departure through the garden, down the path, over the hedge, and into the meadows surrounds him with nature; readers, too, can see themselves within that land. The scene also subtly suggests that Bilbo is appreciating his home's natural appeal before leaving for a potentially permanent journey, and by likening Bilbo leaving to "a rustle of wind," Tolkien positions Bilbo like an inseparable, undisturbing part of nature himself—calm and peaceful as Hobbiton's landscape.

Other images depict the Shire's unique appeal in each season. During the spring when Gandalf returns to reveal the One Ring's true nature to Frodo, Tolkien sets the tone of springtime as Sam leaves the Green Dragon: "It was early April and the sky was now clearing after heavy rain. The sun was down, and a cool pale evening was quietly fading into night. He walked home under the early stars through Hobbiton and up the Hill, whistling softly and thoughtfully."[22] Tolkien provides very specific impressions—the "clearing" sky, the "cool pale evening," the "early stars." Rather than sweeping mountain vistas or breathtaking towers (which readers will experience in other chapters and whose regal qualities I will highlight below), Hobbiton presents rustic, everyday scenes highlighting the "simple pleasures" of life. Tolkien accomplishes this as well when Gandalf and Frodo discuss Sauron's ring: "A bright fire was on the hearth, but the sun was warm, and the wind was in the South. Everything looked fresh, and the new green of Spring was shimmering in the fields and on the tips of the trees' fingers."[23] Springtime in the Shire brings "fresh-ness" and new life, quiet evenings and warm sunlight. Tolkien melds rustic, natural scenes (farms and meadows, gardens and trees) with simple "human" comforts (conversation, good food, celebrations). In such a way, he creates a land to complement its inhabitants and paints a desirable picture for readers. Readers can see again what is familiar; such fantastic recovery positions them to consider why they might want such an appealing place for themselves and perhaps even what steps they would need to take to create such a lifestyle. The Hobbits' agrarian lifestyle suggests a ritualism to their daily existence (caring for the land, reaping its benefits, engaging in close interpersonal relationships) that reinforces the idea of nature as a place of religious connection. Jeffers asserts the Hobbits model a modest relationship with nature that implies almost religious respect: "Hobbits are certainly humble, whether by choice or circumstance, and lead relatively simple lives. They work in tandem with their place to meet their needs, and show reverence for their environment by celebrating its bounties and blessings."[24] Jeffers's language portrays the Hobbits' relationship with the Shire in terms of "reverence" and "blessings," adding to the sense of nature as inherently spiritual, bolstering Tolkien's depictions of numinous nature.

Herbert presents similar "impressionistic" and numinous natural images in describing Arrakis (as well as a potential model for interacting with our own environments, detailed in chapter 3). As with the Shire, Arrakis is both a significant landscape and the setting of most of the first novel's and its sequels' subsequent drama. However, Herbert makes readers consider the power of place even before Paul departs for Arrakis. On Caladan, the Atreides' home planet, Paul contemplates his impending journey and what this new place will mean for him: "He recalled another thing the old woman had said about a world being the sum of many things—the people, the dirt, the growing things, the moons, the tides, the suns—the unknown sum called *nature,* a vague summation without any sense of the *now.* And he wondered: *What is the now?*"[25] Here, Herbert implies that "nature" is unknowable unless experienced directly. Merely presenting it as a concept, a knowable idea, falls short of a "sense of the *now,*" the dynamism of a direct relationship with one's ecosystem. Paul understands this disconnect, and even before entering Arrakis, he prepares himself psychologically to the possibilities of this new environment. This idea hearkens back to the ecocritical activities detailed in the beginning of this chapter, that ecocriticism is distinctive among literary criticism theories because nature is an actual, knowable reality and not only a construct; analyzing a work ecocritically requires readers to consider real-world locales and environmental issues, stretching the reader's experience outside of the fictional world he or she has entered.[26] Meanwhile, back on the pages of *Dune,* Herbert prepares Paul and his readers to experience Arrakis firsthand.

Similarly to the Shire, Arrakis is presented impressionistically (though, to be clear, both the Legendarium and the Duniverse also provide appendices that detail much of Middle-earth and Arrakis's geography, history, and culture). Readers are afforded glimpses of the planet through various characters' points of view. For instance, when Paul's father, the Duke, has a few rare moments of repose, he can see the planet as more than hostile desert: "To the east, the night grew a faggot of luminous gray, then seashell opalescence that dimmed the stars. There came the long, bell-tolling movement of dawn striking across a broken horizon."[27] Herbert's language evokes images both natural and quasi-religious. "Seashell opalescence" ironically contrasts with the surroundings, so far from the presence of bodies of water; "luminous" complements both the "seashell" description and the religious connotations of "long, bell-tolling" coming of the morning, "striking" like a church bell along the "horizon." Such language supports a feeling of reverence and awe induced by the landscape. This moment's splendor is not lost on Leto: "It was a scene of such beauty it caught all his attention. . . . He had never imagined anything here could be as beautiful as that shattered red horizon and purple and ochre cliffs. Beyond the landing field where the night's faint dew had touched life into the hurried seeds of Arrakis, he saw great puddles of red blooms and, running through them, an articulate tread of violet . . . like giant footsteps."[28] Impressions of color combine to give a picture of the land and its majesty: "red," "purple," "ochre," "violet" all call to mind rich, even royal shades. The effect for Leto is one of "beauty" beyond his imagination, not because he was incapable of imagining a beautiful sunrise, but because he could not contextualize it in such a "barren" land. Herbert himself was drawn to the beauty of deserts and other isolated environments: "My father had a lifelong fascination with remote regions of the Earth, from frozen locales to tropics to deserts. Desolate beauty appealed to him . . . the serenity of the wilderness."[29] His depictions here and elsewhere highlight the "serenity" inherent in "desolate" spaces, presenting them as opportunities for characters to be inspired, to reflect upon themselves, to even feel transcendentally affected by them. This experience can extend to his readers, too. Understandably, the Duke has perceived Arrakis as a dangerous home for his family and soldiers, which in many ways it is. However, Herbert also employs a kind of fantastic recovery: we, too, might enter this text inclined to dismiss as ugly or foreign a desert or any natural space that does not conform to our conventional expectations of "beautiful." Through this scene, we can reconsider the beauty, the numinous impact various forms of nature can have on us. Leto, for one, seems changed by this vision: "The Duke nodded, thinking: *Perhaps the planet could grow on one. Perhaps it could become a good home for my son.*"[30] Notwithstanding, he also sees it as potentially "hideous" and dangerous, but that is not the legacy Paul inherits. Paul can move beyond his father's vision to apprehend Arrakis's beauty, even when glorious sunrises do not take place. As we will see, Paul is one of the only nonnative characters in this first novel to see Arrakis as an environment with inherent value, splendor, and power, even separate from the precious spice it produces.

Other descriptions of Arrakis come from characters' conversations about the planet. The Duke, Paul, and Liet-Kynes (the Imperial planetologist and covert Fremen leader) discuss the environmental programs in place on Dune. This conversation reveals how power and money are entangled, and yet the planet itself still exercises ultimate authority: "Kynes darted a hard stare at the Duke. 'Arrakis could be an Eden if its rulers would look up from grubbing for spice!' . . . 'How is a planet to become an Eden without money?' 'What is money,' Kynes asked, 'if it won't buy the services you need? . . . Some parts of the desert teem with life. But all of it has learned how to survive under these rigors. If *you* get caught down there, you imitate that life or you die.'"[31] This passage operates on two levels: First, it implies that in its current state, Arrakis requires adaptation from humans, not the other way around. Like the Shire, the land is its own force of nature, not simply a passive object; each place has its own distinct history and life, separate from the people who do and will inhabit them. Arrakis and Middle-earth take on the significance of characters themselves, exacting their own requirements. And in the case of Arrakis, failure to "imitate that life" in the desert is a question of survival, of existence itself. Talk of money and power, though important, pales in comparison to the awe of this planet's demands. On another level, this passage implies a sense of fantastic recovery—readers can project their own planet's welfare onto Arrakis's; if Arrakis could be transformed into a paradise "if its rulers would look up from grubbing for spice," the implication is that Earth could be environmentally transformed if its own leaders had the concern to invest in the planet's future environmental security.

While at times Paul faces fear and intimidation in the desert because of its "rigors" (a harsh landscape, deadly sandworms, the need for new survival skills), he quickly begins to appreciate the desert's inherent contradictions, its simultaneous capacity for great danger and great majesty. Paul's apprehension at encountering a sandworm in the open desert is lightened by a sunrise, echoing his father's earlier view of another sunrise (and narratively poignant, as his father has recently been betrayed and murdered at the hands of the Harkonnens): "In that instant, the sun lifted above the horizon somewhere to the left beyond the end of the fissure. Colors blinked in the sand out on the open desert. A chorus of birds held forth their songs from hidden places among the rocks."[32] Combining colors and birdsong to create a lovely moment of reflection, Herbert pairs scenes of danger with those of a nature that in some ways is beyond violence. The land exists as it is, not malicious or consciously harmful, though by its very nature it can be dangerous to humans. In many of these passages, the reader's perspective of the desert is affected by the situations in which the characters are placed; as the characters progress in adapting to the planet and its needs, they begin to apprehend themselves as part of the planet and see its beauty and value in its own right.[33] Leto and Paul are at times less aware of this beauty because of their stressful circumstances, yet when they have the respite to reflect on their environments, they begin to rethink what the desert holds. Like the Shire, though so very geologically different from each other, these spaces encourage readers to see beauty in small, ordinary moments of nature—birds singing, gardens growing, life existing in its various forms—yet these ordinary moments carry an appeal almost spiritual in quality.

Like Leto and Paul, Jessica too comes to see the appeal in Arrakis's landscape. Herbert juxtaposes two different impressions: Jessica's memory of Caladan's beauty, and the majesty of a spice worm's appearance. As readers see throughout *The Lord of the Rings,* different images of nature are not necessarily presented as better than one another, but rather Tolkien shows value in different kinds of natural spaces. These scenes also suggest that readers should not let their prior conceptions about nature inhibit them from seeing nature's value in its many forms. For example, Herbert shares Jessica's memory of Caladan's attraction: "She closed her eyes and, against this wasteland, conjured in her mind a scene from Caladan. There had been a vacation trip once on Caladan. . . . They'd flown over the southern jungles, above the weed-wild shouting leaves and rice paddies of the deltas. And they had seen the ant lines in the greenery—man-gangs carrying their loads on suspensor-buoyed shoulder poles. And in the sea reaches there'd been the white petals of trimaran dhows. All of it gone."[34] The images above give readers a sense of why Leto and Jessica find life on Arrakis so challenging—it is so unlike the lush "jungles," "leaves," and "greenery" of Caladan. Jessica uses these memories as a retreat, a way of denying the harsh land she is traversing and the unknown dangers ahead of her. It might be tempting for readers to adopt this escapist attitude as well; we can sympathize with Jessica's need to avoid this strange, barren desert. And yet, Herbert subverts the comforts of Jessica's escape. Moments after her reminiscences, she and Paul see a worm up close for the first time, an experience not without its own splendor and awe:

> It came from their right with an uncaring majesty that could not be ignored. A twisting burrow-mound of sand cut through the dunes within their field of vision. The mound lifted in front, dusting away like a bow wave in water. Then it was gone, coursing off to the left. . . . Where the worm had passed there remained that tantalizing gap. It flowed bitterly endless before them, beckoning beneath its horizontal collapse of skyline. . . . [Paul] looked at his hand. How inadequate it appeared when measured against such creatures as that worm.[35]

The worm's "uncaring majesty," likened to the enormity of a ship traveling through the sand "waves," echoes the "dhows" in the "sea reaches" on Caladan. While Jessica prefers Caladan, Herbert's descriptions suggest a parallel, equal value in both locations. Moreover, the spice worm's appearance prompts an existential reaction from Paul. His own insignificance and "inadequacy" in the face of the worm's presence suggests the kind of ecocritical thinking referenced in the last chapter—an animism that calls into question anthropocentric ideology. The sandworms do more than exist; they have a life and strength to them that puts Paul's own existence and concerns into a different perspective. The sandworms, too, contribute to the land's feeling of religious awe, further supporting its numinous impact on Herbert's readers. In addition, as will be explored below, the animist and anthropomorphic elements in these stories also contribute to the mythopoeic and ecocritical effects outlined in chapter 1.

Other desert impressions guide readers through Herbert's world-building and reinforce the near-mythical feel of Arrakis. After the Duke's capture, Jessica and Paul escape through the desert, which becomes a series of trials for them as they deal with a new, unpredictable environment and Paul becomes more aware of his prophetic abilities. Through these tests, mother and son begin to become acquainted with the desert as the Fremen know it—as its own force, active and dangerous, demanding respect but also a beautiful land. They experience the desert through a combination of fatigue, fear, and awe at its strangeness: "She [Jessica] followed the shadowy movement of Paul's progress, . . . onto a shallow, moonlit basin. Paul stepped out into the rim of the basin, whispered: 'What a beautiful place.' Jessica could only stare in silent agreement from her position a step behind him."[36] This scene is filled with images of "moonlight" and "beautiful" growing things, "bushes, cacti, tiny clumps of leaves—all trembling in the moonlight."[37] Paul claims it is like a "fairyland," and Jessica sees the basin as "moonfrosted." Herbert's language here is a delicate balance of light and dark,[38] wasteland and tiny oasis. The effect is that of an enchanted place, something that has managed to survive even in the face of danger and difficult living conditions. Another scene during Paul and Jessica's desert escape shows readers various sensory impressions. Paul notices a mouse being caught by a bird, reflecting on the vulnerability of those in the desert: "Paul continued to stare across the basin. He inhaled, sensed the softly cutting contralto smell of sage climbing the night. The predatory bird—he thought of it as the way of this desert. It had brought a stillness to the basin so unuttered that the blue-milk moonlight could almost be heard flowing across sentinel saguaro and spiked paintbrush. There was a low humming of light here more basic in its harmony than any other music in his universe."[39] This passage is filled with carefully selected sensory appeals: Paul *smells* the desert scent, interestingly described as a sound and a smell: contralto is a low female singing voice, and here it brings the odor of sage (a healing plant, ironically from the Latin for "safe"). He *sees* the bird, and then notices the silence. The moonlight can "almost be heard"—again, an interesting linking of sight and sound in a nonlogical connection. Paul senses a "humming light" that creates harmony. The effect of this language is of a strange, totally immersive experience, perhaps numinous: similar to that mood of fantasy and enchantment Tolkien has defined in "On Fairy-Stories," and also reminiscent of Tolkien's descriptions of the Shire's beauty.

Though the planet Arrakis undergoes many changes over the millennia that span these chronicles, Herbert never fails to depict it as beautiful and valuable. As Paul sees the impact of his environmental plan taking effect in *Dune Messiah,* Herbert pairs an interesting reflection on how the land impacts him as both Fremen and as someone trying to transform the planet: "Moonlight slanted down into an enclosed garden, sentinel trees and broad leaves, wet foliage. He could see a fish pond reflecting stars among the leaves, pockets of white floral brilliance in the shadows. Momentarily, he saw the garden through Fremen eyes: alien, menacing, dangerous in its waste of water."[40] This passage is a way for readers to see how Arrakis has changed in the years since the first novel concluded; however, it also reframes nature and identifies real concerns: use versus waste, consumerism versus conservation. (Some of these environmental concerns will be picked up later in this study.) Herbert continues his juxtaposition of beautiful and dangerous images; for most readers, the "wet foliage" and the "fish pond reflecting stars among the leaves" sound quite appealing, but for Paul, he cannot remove his desert experiences from his new lifestyle. Descriptions here and later show beauty and protection for Paul and those around him, but they also show a larger picture of the planet's resources. While Paul and the Fremen find ways to increase these resources, Paul keeps Fremen values at heart, mistrusting the "waste of water" that such a new, lavish lifestyle demands. He is ever aware of how tentative his "control" over the planet is: "This planet beneath him which he had commanded be remade from desert into a water-rich paradise, it was alive. It had a pulse as dynamic as that of any human. It fought him, resisted, slipped away from his commands."[41] Herbert is sure to remind readers that Arrakis exists despite Paul's leadership, despite the Fremen, despite any interference; Herbert is similarly reminding readers that our own planet is "alive" with its own "dynamic pulse," as deserving of our respect and care as Arrakis is of Paul's (and as Tolkien has done with Middle-earth).[42]

In the third Dune novel, the desert has shrunk to half its original size, and much of its original beauty is lost, too. Herbert continues to pair the two sides of the planet—a dangerous "greening" as the environmental transformation continues, and the rugged appeal of the original desert (though I would hasten to add that Herbert does not overtly condemn the environmental change per se; rather, he frames the desert in such a way as to assert its value and imply that there is something implicitly worthwhile in unaltered nature).[43] Paul's sister Alia, left in command after Paul wanders blind into the desert, cannot help but return to the Fremen visions of the desert: "In her mind, as in the minds of all Fremen, the ocean-desert still held Dune in a grip which would never relax. She had only to close her eyes and she would see that desert."[44] Like many of the Atreides, Alia seeks out the desert for reflection: "It would be twilight soon and . . . there would come a special quality of evening which few places in the universe could match. It would be that softly lighted desert world with its persistent solitude, its saturated sense that each creature in it was alone in a new universe."[45] As the novels progress, Herbert frequently pairs images of the desert with a character's spiritual experience. The desert's "persistent solitude" that creates a mood of a "new universe" shows readers how stark yet profound the landscape can be. By the fourth novel, as Paul's son Leto II has merged with the environment to become a hybrid human/sandworm himself, the desert is being reclaimed. Herbert's descriptions here again evoke the unique beauty of the desert, as Leto II looks out at the fields and greenery that are slowly being transformed:

> The fields of the Royal Plantations reached outward beyond the forest and, when the sun lifted over the far curve of land, it beamed glowing gold across grain rippling in the fields. The grain reminded Leto of sand, of sweeping dunes which once had marched across this very ground.
>   *And will march once more.*[46]

Because the planet's ecological transformation is reversed, Leto II can preserve the Fremen's desire for desert land. Yet, Herbert subverts readers' expectations about nature. Instead of describing the "gold" grain fields as desirable places of life and growth, the author links this image to the "sweeping dunes" that "will march once more"—the endless sand from Paul's days will return and bring back the Fremen lifestyle. Herbert does not condemn the grainfields, but he does depict the desert in such a way as to promote appreciation for it. The desert, worms, and water scarcity combine to give the Fremen a reverent attitude toward their natural world. One of the Fremen sayings from Liet-Kynes shows this religious awe: "'Bless the Maker and His Water. . . . Bless the coming and going of Him, May His passing cleanse the world. May He keep the world for His people.'"[47] Herbert has built nature's religious quality into the plot of the novels, but he builds these plots and imagined places so convincingly as to potentially give them real-world weight. Readers, too, can think of the numinous potential of the desert. After all, over the course of the six novels, readers are not left with a green, lush Dune—they are left with a desert; even after Dune is destroyed and the Bene Gesserit retreat to their home planet, Chapterhouse, the Sisters begin to convert their own climate to a desert. Besides supporting these stories' plots, Herbert suggests that the desert is what endures and is worthy of being preserved. In essence, both Tolkien and Herbert give primacy to the landscapes they describe.

Trees and Worms: Anthropomorphic, Zoomorphic, and Allomorphic Nature

By portraying nature as beautiful, inviting, and valuable, Tolkien and Herbert are engaged in the work of mythopoeic fantasists. They provide a refreshing escape into enthralling and now-iconic Secondary worlds like the Shire and Arrakis; indeed, Curry notes an "uncanny feeling, shared by many of [Tolkien's] readers, of actually having been there [Middle-earth], and knowing it from the inside, rather than simply having read about it."[48] The same can be said of the Duniverse. In addition to comprehensive world-building, Tolkien and Herbert encourage readers to recover an appreciation for the Primary World's natural beauty. Part of this appreciation is achieved by foregrounding nature in their fantasy texts, detailed in many of the charming, impressionistic passages cited above. The authors also unite Secondary and Primary worlds through "hybridized" anthropomorphic, zoomorphic, and allomorphic depictions of such creatures as talking trees and giant sandworms. In Garrard's treatment of Animal Studies, the author delineates several different ways of "looking at" or "seeing ourselves" in representations of animals. Among these are "critical anthropomorphism" ("employing the language and concepts of human behaviour 'carefully, consciously, empathetically, and biocentrically'"[49] to animals), a representation of likeness (metonymy); "critical zoomorphism" (in opposition to "crude zoomorphism," which "depends in turn upon a prior, crudely anthropomorphic projection of despised human qualities onto . . . animals"[50]), which while also representing likeness does so by placing animal qualities onto the nonanimal; and allomorphism (Garrard's neologism that characterizes "the wondrous strangeness of animals, which often involves an overtly sacred language"[51]), a representation of "numinous" otherness.[52] The effect of this hybridization is twofold: it creates that mood of enchantment that Tolkien explained in "On Fairy-Stories," introducing new and fantastic creatures; in addition, it disrupts readers' preconceived ideas of what is human and nonhuman, thus potentially shifting the boundaries between humanity and nature, therefore challenging our tendency to "other" nature.[53]

Probably the most iconic anthropomorphized creatures in the Legendarium are the Ents, though Tolkien introduces sentient trees before the fellowship even forms.[54] The Hobbits journey through the landscapes surrounding the Shire, making their way into the Old Forest. Here, Tolkien details the variety of trees in the forest and its atmosphere. Merry recently gave the Hobbits a history of the forest and how the Hobbits abused it, in turn invoking the forest's ill will. Against this uneasy backdrop, the Hobbits venture forward, almost oppressively surrounded by the trees: "Looking ahead they could see only tree-trunks of innumerable sizes and shapes: straight or bent, twisted, leaning, squat or slender, smooth or gnarled and branched; and all the stems were green or grey with moss and slimy, shaggy growths."[55] In this chapter, Tolkien joins together the familiar and the novel, human-like characteristics and trees (as Brawley has explained, this amalgam reinforces readers' sense of fantastic "recovery," which is accentuated even more so with the Ents). By providing the strained history of the Old Forest and the Hobbits, Tolkien makes the four Hobbits and readers more sensitive to the trees' human-like features, certainly adding a tenseness to the scenes that follow. This anthropomorphizing also makes the descriptions of the trees more significant—they evoke the variety and uniqueness of people, as they come in all "sizes and shapes," and these sizes and shapes sound like human bodies in their idiosyncrasies. And, while these trees do not move and speak in the direct, recognizable ways the Ents do, they still exert a tangible influence on their "trespassers," reframing themselves as active participants in their environment instead of passive objects that the Hobbits can avoid or engage with as desired.

The travelers feel this influence as they move through the Forest:[56] "They picked a way among the trees, and their ponies plodded along, carefully avoiding the many writhing and interlacing roots. There was no undergrowth. The ground was rising steadily, and as they went forward it seemed that the trees became taller, darker, and thicker. There was no sound, except an occasional drip of moisture falling through the still leaves."[57] Tolkien carefully builds the tension in this scene, taking readers from a sense of unease among the "writhing and interlacing roots," language that evokes a feeling of menace,[58] as if the roots are purposefully trying to tangle the Hobbits, and the eerie silence, broken only by a "drip of moisture falling through the still leaves." These very specific images and sounds place readers in the characters' circumstances in a believable way, as if we too are in this dramatic scene. Tolkien continues building tension in the Old Forest: "For the moment there was no whispering or movement among the branches; but they all got an uncomfortable feeling that they were being watched with disapproval, deepening to dislike and even enmity. The feeling steadily grew, until they found themselves looking up quickly, or glancing back over their shoulders, as if they expected a sudden blow."[59] Within a few lines, we see the characters slip into a state of mild paranoia, as if they are "being watched," and the oppressive feeling of the forest begins to exert its influence on us, as well. We can almost sense the same "dislike and even enmity" on our protagonists, or even on us, as we trespass through the forest with the Hobbits. Pippin succumbs to the fear, calling out, and the forest's response is no more encouraging than the prior passages implied: "The cry fell as if muffled by a heavy curtain. There was no echo or answer though the wood seemed to become more crowded and more watchful than before."[60] Readers can picture the "crowded" trees looming over the Hobbits. However, even though Frodo thinks the woods "abominable," as readers we can also feel a certain amount of sympathy for why the forest is so hostile. Tolkien is not necessarily implying that this is an outright evil woods (at least not yet), but instead it is like the rest of the people and places in Middle-earth—complicated, nuanced, flawed, acting from and for its own self-preservation:[61] "What Tolkien was trying to convey was something both supernatural and spiritual that he felt was important for the world to know. His tree-fairy and his tree-characters are archaic yet tenacious, ancient yet curiously vital manifestations of a mythic world of sentient nature. This is a world that is, as he said in his *Beowulf* essay, 'alive at once and in all its parts,' a world aware of itself and us, not only watching us but interacting with us and affecting us, if we only knew it. Tolkien knew it."[62] Tolkien's depiction of trees complicates our typical view of nature as passive or unconscious.[63] As much as this is an exciting and dangerous part of the story, Tolkien is offering a view of nature that animates it with human characteristics; because of the Hobbits and the Old Forest's history, Tolkien is placing these two groups into similar positions of blame and responsibility. Thus, these scenes can potentially put readers into an ecocritical mindset—we might reconsider what responsibility we have to the trees or land around us, and how what we might judge as inconvenient or unnecessary encroachment of nature is merely nature trying to survive as humans encroach upon nature's land, as Dickerson and Evans have also argued.[64]

The forest also has a sense of enchantment to it—it creates a heavy, hot atmosphere that demoralizes the Hobbits and preys upon their uncertainty in undertaking the journey. By linking the forest with magical powers, as well as anthropomorphizing it, Tolkien imbues this place with more than just a passive influence. The land has power and agency to react to its circumstances, sometimes in manipulative ways. Indeed, the Hobbits soon lose their way, as the forest seems to lead them down and into the heart of the woods. And yet, even in what becomes a perilous stage in their journey (as the woods begin to consume them while they fall into an enchanted nap), there is a certain amount of beauty to be appreciated, suggesting that nature in the Secondary World, as in the Primary World, maintains contradictions. The protagonists emerge from the confusing gullies onto a vista: "A golden afternoon of late sunshine lay warm and drowsy upon the hidden land between. In the midst of it there wound lazily a dark river of brown water, bordered with ancient willows, arched over with willows, blocked with fallen willows, and flecked with thousands of faded willow-leaves. The air was thick with them, fluttering yellow from the branches; for there was a warm and gentle breeze blowing softly in the valley, and the reeds were rustling, and the willow-boughs were creaking."[65] While Old Man Willow does emerge as a dangerous, arguably malicious force,[66] Tolkien has painted a memorable, beautiful scene of richly colored sensory impressions: "golden" light, a "dark" and "brown" river, and the air filled with the yellow of the willow trees, almost overwhelmingly so, as well as the soft sounds of the "rustling" reeds and the "creaking" boughs. No menace is present here, just a striking moment of near-peacefulness among all the strange and stressful moments the forest has created thus far. This scene takes on a dream-like quality, reminiscent of some of the beauty Tolkien imbued the Shire with in earlier chapters. It provides both characters and readers with a restorative vision—not all trees are menacing and vengeful.

Herbert, too, uses hybridization in the Duniverse to blend the human and nonhuman. One of the most significant features of the landscape are the sandworms. Calling to mind mythical dragons guarding treasures (in this case, they are the source of the spice, which each group of people desires for its own motives), these creatures are not portrayed as solely hideous or villainous. Instead, Herbert presents them as almost reverent creatures (akin to Garrard's neologism, "allomorphism"). As mentioned before, Herbert compares the worms to massive ships, regal and awe-inspiring. Even Paul knows that the worms are more than desert "monsters": "Paul studied the open desert, questing in his prescient memory, probing the mysterious allusions to thumpers and maker hooks in the Fremkit manual that had come with their escape pack. He found it odd that all he sensed was pervasive terror at thought of the worms. He knew as though it lay just at the edge of his awareness that the worms were to be respected and not feared . . . if . . . if."[67] Paul's prescience (spice-augmented prophetic visions) develops the longer he is on Arrakis, enhancing his ability to see the future, his connection with nature, and his ability to recognize the desert's beauty and value, including the worms, for its own sake. Paul begins to sense the "respect" these creatures deserve rather than "pervasive terror"; he is able to sort out the cognitive dissonance between this terror and a reenvisioning of these worms. The "if" is how the Fremen have learned to ride these great creatures, traveling deeper into the desert to reclaim moisture, which in turn helps to create "little makers" (the infant phase of sandworm development) and thus perpetuating the health and success of the sandworms. Through these creatures, Herbert is modeling a symbiotic, cyclical relationship between humans and sandworm, overseeing one another's life cycles.[68]

In fact, Herbert goes even further in depicting the sandworms as significant creatures. The Fremen refer to fully grown worms as "Shai-Hulud," which Herbert explains to mean "the 'Old Man of the Desert,' 'Old Father Eternity,' and 'Grandfather of the Desert.' Significantly, this name, when referred to in a certain tone or written with capital letters, designates the earth deity of Fremen hearth superstition."[69] For the Fremen, the sandworms have a spiritual significance (partially because they produce the spice that augments their religious ceremonies); while Paul and Jessica see these beliefs as "hearth superstition," the language Herbert employs to describe the worms and the characters' interactions with them evokes a sense of their allomorphic numinosity—they are creatures older and more powerful than the human characters, representative perhaps of a greater force, something outside of the Fremen.[70] And, of course, their use in rituals (the spice-induced visions, their teeth as "crysknives" used in ritual battle, the little makers drowned in water to create the water used to test Bene Gesserit) also add a sense of the mystical to them. Like the desert itself, the sandworms contribute to nature's numinous qualities, encouraging readers to apprehend their own environments as similarly divine.

Perhaps the most obvious and important hybridization Herbert employs comes in *God Emperor of Dune*, as Leto II has merged with the sandtrout (infant sandworms) and over the course of millennia transformed himself into a part-human/part-sandworm creature (something between anthropomorphism and zoomorphism). To save Dune from Paul's perhaps too-hasty terraforming, Leto is returning the planet to a desert landscape and the lifestyle that goes with this desert. As chapter 3 analyzes in greater detail, the Fremen who evolved from the "greened" Dune lack much of the moral strength of their ancestors; the "soft" environment creates a morally soft people, and the trials of the harsh desert no longer exist to challenge the Fremen. Whether for better or worse, Leto II enacts his Golden Path, the slow return of the desert as well as a difficult example for humanity of what happens when power and control are centralized. Through his actions, Leto knowingly causes his own destruction, but all subsequent sandworms now carry a bit of him, a small piece of human consciousness. Leto's evolution into a sentient sandworm adds to this breakdown of "other-ness," as the boundary between human and nonhuman blurs.[71] Moreover, by associating the sandworms with treasure (mélange spice), Herbert not only draws upon mythological material (Greek mythology and *Beowulf* among them) but also suggests these creatures are valuable in and of themselves. As an inextricable part of the spice-creation cycle, the worms are more than just monsters to be conquered; they possess an intrinsic value and are worth protecting and preserving. Like Tolkien's depiction of trees, they present dangers, but they respond based upon survival, a self-preservation akin to the Old Forest and Old Man Willow. The sandworms are not less worthy of characters' care and respect because of these dangers. They are not as "other" as readers may at first believe.

Rivendell and Lothlórien, Chapterhouse and Gondor: Regal Nature

Tolkien and Herbert employ fantastic recovery throughout their various depictions of nature, including the landscapes where Elves, Men, and the Bene Gesserit abide. Here, the authors show a nature that has been shaped by its inhabitants. While still beautiful and even awe-inspiring, these spaces differ from the others (the Shire, Arrakis, the Old Forest) in that they have been altered in such a way as to conform to these communities' ideals of beauty and function. The Elves and the Bene Gesserit, especially, change their environments by ordering and "enhancing" them into more aesthetically pleasing spaces. While the next chapter will address more directly what this enhancement reveals about the characters' attitudes toward nature, both authors are presenting a variety of natural places and suggesting something about human interactions with nature. Unlike the earlier glimpses of nature found in the Shire and Arrakis, these places take on more regal descriptions. They also lack some of the hybridized features of the Old Forest and the sandworms; these environments seem to stay in the realm of nature-as-other, in the sense that the characters living in these spaces utilize them for their own purposes (albeit mostly positive ones), carefully shaping them to fit their needs. The intention in this section is not to condemn the fact that these environments have been altered, but rather to show that Tolkien and Herbert fill their mythopoeic worlds with nature in many forms, each of which can be appreciated and cared for in much the same way our own abundant variety of natural spaces can be.

Part way through *The Fellowship of the Ring*, the company makes its way to Rivendell, in which Tolkien provides the first Elven environment (beyond a brief earlier encounter). Rivendell is clearly a place of enchantment and power, though of a different kind than the other places—more influenced by the people rather than the land itself; Elrond exerts power over the river, the home, the valley. Here, the land reflects the character of the people. Frodo experiences rest through Rivendell's peacefulness, which is surrounded by nature: "Sam led him along several passages and down many steps and out into a high garden above the steep bank of the river. He found his friends sitting in a porch on the side of the house looking east. Shadows had fallen in the valley below, but there was still a light on the faces of the mountains far above. The air was warm. The sound of running and falling water was loud, and the evening was filled with a faint scent of trees and flowers, as if summer still lingered in Elrond's gardens."[72] Like Hobbiton, Rivendell has natural features that make it appealing to its visitors; however, there is a sense of height and grandness that the Shire lacks; they are near the "faces of the mountains," with "running and falling water" filling the air, and the "scent of trees and flowers" imply an almost enchanted summertime, outside of the regular passage of time and seasons. The Elves have exerted their own mystical powers over this place, evoking a sense of the ethereal that Hobbiton does not share. If the appeal of the Shire is its ordinariness and the desert its solitude, Rivendell has an otherworldly draw (as scholars like Campbell, Dickerson and Evans, and others have acknowledged).[73] Tolkien builds on this sense of otherworldly beauty: "[Frodo] walked along the terraces above the loud-flowing Bruinen and watched the pale, cool sun rise above the far mountains, and shine down, slanting through the thin silver mist; the dew upon the yellow leaves was glimmering, and the woven nets of gossamer twinkled on every bush. Sam walked beside him, saying nothing, but sniffing the air, and looking every now and again with wonder in his eyes at the great heights in the East. The snow was white upon their peaks."[74] The language Tolkien uses suggests precious metals or pale colors: "the pale, cool sun," "thin silver mist," the "glimmering" dew on "yellow leaves," probably creating a golden effect, "gossamer twinkled," and "white" snowy mountain tops. The terraced buildings in Rivendell produce "wonder" in Frodo and Sam, offering new vistas of awe and delight, which Lothlórien will also exhibit. Rich, earthy colors of green, red, and yellow filled the Shire, while more delicate colors belong to the Elves. The Elves fill their lands with aesthetically altered buildings to fit their landscapes, such that a reader might even feel their habitations are like houses of worship—beautified to extol the splendor of nature.

Lothlórien is another place showcasing the ethereal beauty of Middle-earth. Like Rivendell, the Elves have enhanced their natural surroundings according to their aesthetic tastes, but unlike Rivendell, Lothlórien has even more mysterious qualities, harkening back to a mythic time. These descriptions of nature are perhaps some of the most important in the Legendarium as they resonated emotionally with Tolkien in a unique way: "The chapter on Lothlórien is, perhaps, the most moving chapter in relation to the love of the earth itself; in fact, it was the chapter that moved Tolkien the most, and he felt that the chapter had been written by someone else."[75] In part, Tolkien believed Lothlórien had such beauty because the trees were well loved.[76] Legolas paints a visual for readers of the woods, describing some of that profound love, beauty, and wonder:[77] "'There lie the woods of Lothlórien!' said Legolas. 'That is the fairest of all the dwellings of my people. There are no trees like the trees of that land. For in the autumn their leaves fall not, but turn to gold. Not till the spring comes and the new green opens do they fall, and then the boughs are laden with yellow flowers; and the floor of the wood is golden, and golden is the roof, and its pillars are of silver, for the bark of the trees is smooth and grey.'"[78] The imagery here is repeated in *The Silmarillion,* as the trees and colors reflect Middle-earth's earliest geography. And the magic of these early days, when demigods walked among Elves and Men, lingers still in Lothlórien. Tolkien's language depicts nature as royal: the leaves "turn to gold," the wood's "pillars are of silver," its roof and floor are also "golden," and there are rich greens and yellows.[79] Much of this imagery is repeated and even improved upon as the characters encounter the woods for the first time. The woods have a mysterious, magical quality for the companions, and none of them leaves unchanged. Each member is impacted by its unearthly splendor; in fact, the experience for Gimli is one that contributes to a breakdown of his "power from" relationship with nature.[80] And Frodo's reaction is one of "wonder" surpassing an ordinary experience: "The fact that Frodo looks on the scene with 'wonder' suggests the connection with fantasy critics' defining element of 'wonder' as the core of the genre, that feeling-oriented experience which is also undefinable."[81] Brawley claims the scenes in Lothlórien powerfully illustrate the unique effects of mythopoeic fantasy and numinous nature. Through fantastic recovery, Tolkien uses Lothlórien as a means of conveying "the world not as it *is*, but as it was *meant* to be seen; it is a recovery of a sacramental vision";[82] in addition, Brawley maintains that "this indescribable quality of a felt experience is exactly that of the numinous consciousness."[83] In short, Lothlórien is yet another example of the inherent divinity of nature, quite literally true of those woods, but also true in a different sense in the Primary World.

Through his depiction of Lothlórien, Tolkien portrays the transcendent qualities of nature. The natural world allows these characters to see themselves and their world anew. Thus, it becomes a model for readers: even if we cannot recreate the mystical qualities of Lothlórien in our own world, we can find the transformative power of our environment. As Sam observes, the Elves have found a sense of self in their lands: "They seem to belong here, more even than Hobbits do in the Shire. Whether they've made the land, or the land's made them, it's hard to say. . . . It's wonderfully quiet here. Nothing seems to be going on, and nobody seems to want it to. If there's any magic about, it's right down deep, where I can't lay my hands on it."[84] Clearly, nature exists for the Elves as both beautiful and functional, a home that they have made or been made by, with a mysterious "magical" pull that resists quantification or categorization. Theirs is a lifestyle that values quality of existence, enriched by nature's ethereal beauty. This passage also calls to mind Lewis's views as a "romantic rationalist"—he trusted in external nature as a way to the divine and transcendent as much as truth and reality are ways to the divine and transcendent. Tolkien's depiction of nature is in line with this perspective—nature is not presented as merely a place to appreciate, though it is that, too. It is part of a lifestyle, a symbiotic relationship between person and place. As Brawley observes, "Perceiving this sacred dimension of Middle-earth is life-affirming and involves what Curry views as a sensual appreciation for *this* world."[85] While readers can get lost in the stories Tolkien and Herbert create, a profounder connection with nature is also a powerful potential of our reading experiences, via fantastic escape and recovery. This escape portrays healthful relationships with nature, not simply nature as "other": "Such an appreciation for nature is a view of nature as part of a community, not as a commodity. This involves an appreciation of nature as it is, not for how it can be used. Tolkien had this in mind in many of his scenes involving nature."[86] Tolkien gives readers the opportunity to embrace such an appreciation, to have a close connection to the Earth as valuable in and of itself, and to recognize the interconnections between each other and our land, our inseparable ecosystems. This is idealistic but not unrealistic. As Haldir tells Merry, "'The world is indeed full of peril, and in it there are many dark places; but still there is much that is fair, and though in all lands love is now mingled with grief, it grows perhaps the greater.'"[87] Through recovery, escape, and consolation, readers of fantasy can enter into a new apprehension of their interpersonal and environmental choices, and even of their spiritual existence.

Perhaps similar to the Elves, the desire to "enhance" people and places is at the core of the Bene Gesserit, the religious sisterhood of the Duniverse. Their home planet, Chapterhouse, is almost monastic in its cultivation of gardens and orchards. The Bene Gesserit use their environments (or at least this part of Chapterhouse; the Sisterhood has many planets that are used for various purposes) for meditative spaces, or to teach lessons about the work they do, which they describe as cultivating people. As such, they are typically calming, aesthetically pleasing spaces, attractive but also functional:

> Deep in the orchard, they listened quietly for a time to birds and insects. Bees working the clover of a nearby pasture came to investigate ... They buzzed past him, sensed identifiers and went away about their business with blossoms.... On a morning walk near harvest time in his [Teg's] ninth year, just over the third rise in the apple orchards north of Central, they came on a shallow depression free of trees and lush with many different plants. Odrade put a hand on his shoulder and held him where they could admire black stepping-stones in a meander track through massed greenery and tiny flowers.[88]

The orchard houses improved nature: "blossoms," "plants," "stepping-stones" placed for visitors to admire the "massed greenery and tiny flowers." The purpose of the gardens and orchards is to be admired for the work that the Sisterhood has done in creating such beautiful landscapes. These spaces are not preserved for their natural charms alone but rather tirelessly maintained through generations of care and alterations: "Seeds and young shoots had been brought here on the original no-ships some fifteen hundred years ago, she said, and had been planted with loving care. Teg visualized hands grubbing in dirt, gently patting earth around young shoots, careful irrigation, the fencing to confine the cattle to wild pastures around the first Chapterhouse plantations and buildings."[89] Unlike the Shire, where agriculture is practiced as both survival and a way to be closer to the land, Chapterhouse's agricultural practices must also fulfill a sense of beauty, proportion, and function. The control the Bene Gesserit value so much is evidenced in their environments,[90] and, like Tolkien, Herbert is not necessarily privileging this environmental care over Paul's or the Fremen's; rather, readers can see a different model of how to relate to the environment, one that values nature's aesthetic qualities but which can lead to a spiritual connection no less than the other relationships.

Other examples of environments that show the distinct presence of their inhabitants include Rohan and Gondor, which represent the alterations of Men on nature. In *The Two Towers*, the disbanded company now travels in different directions throughout Middle-earth. Aragorn, Legolas, and Gimli pursue the captured Merry and Pippin, searching the lands of Rohan for clues. Despite the horrific conditions they have just left (especially Boromir's death), they are presented with scenes of natural beauty:

> Turning back they saw across the River the far hills kindled. Day leaped into the sky. The red rim of the sun rose over the shoulders of the dark land. Before them in the West the world lay still, formless and grey; but even as they looked, the shadows of night melted, the colours of the waking earth returned: green flowed over the wide meads of Rohan; the white mists shimmered in the water-vales; and far off to the left, thirty leagues or more, blue and purple, stood the White Mountains, rising into peaks of jet, tipped with glimmering snows, flushed with the rose of morning.[91]

Tolkien uses such passages to provide an immersive sensory experience of nature's splendor. It is almost as if the Earth brings such renewal to remind them that grief and sadness will pass away, just as the "shadows of night melted." "Waking earth" brings hope, life, and an abundance of colorful vitality: "green," "white," "blue and purple," "the rose of morning." The beauty of this scene prompts longing in Aragorn, as he wishes he could go to the mountains of his home in Gondor. In addition, Tolkien's use of color to describe this scene echoes the language that will be used again to describe Rohan and later Gondor.

After the characters travel to Théoden's hall in Rohan, they discover how Wormtongue has deceived and enchanted Théoden, allowing the Rohirrim to sit by idly as Saruman destroys Fanghorn Forest and marshals evil forces. Gandalf breaks the enchantment in a dramatic moment that highlights nature as a powerful force:

> "Now, lord," said Gandalf, "look out upon your land! Breathe the free air again!"
> From the porch upon the top of the high terrace they could see beyond the stream the green fields of Rohan fading into distant grey. Curtains of wind-blown rain were slanting down. The sky above and to the west was still dark with thunder, and lightning far away flickered among the tops of hidden hills. But the wind had shifted to the north, and already the storm that had come out of the East was receding, rolling away southward to the sea. Suddenly through a rent in the clouds behind them a shaft of sun stabbed down. The falling showers gleamed like silver, and far away the river flittered like a shimmering glass.[92]

As before, Tolkien utilizes colors and descriptions of nature to provide an impression of power, majesty, and beauty. Like Rivendell, Rohan has lofty, terraced portions, allowing its guests views of the "green fields" that stretch for miles around. The ominous weather adds to the tone of this scene—like Théoden, it is dark and moody: the sky is "dark with thunder," as lightning flashes around "hidden hills." Yet, Gandalf breaks the curse on Théoden, and the weather breaks, too, "rolling away southward to the sea." Théoden and readers are left with a vision of a powerful beam of light that "stabbed down," and the remaining rainfall appears "silver," the river "like a shimmering glass." Nature is strong and regal, and by pairing the shift in weather with Gandalf's magical abilities, Tolkien again imbues nature with the potential to be more than inert object. He offers a fantastic reenvisioning of a seemingly mundane activity (light coming through a passing storm), providing readers with an impactful scene of nature's transformation into a force as breathtaking as Gandalf's wizardry.

Gondor, too, is filled with royal language and sensory impressions.[93] *The Return of the King* opens with descriptions of Minas Tirith. It is a man-made place, but it celebrates beauty in both humankind and nature. Pippin's first glimpses of the royal city provide a sense of its glory:

> Even as Pippin gazed in wonder the walls passed from looming grey to white, blushing faintly in the dawn; and suddenly the sun climbed over the eastern shadow and sent forth a shaft that smote the face of the City. Then Pippin cried aloud, for the Tower of Ecthelion, standing high within the topmost wall, shone out against the sky, glimmering like a spike of pearl and silver, tall and fair and shapely, and its pinnacle glittered as if it were wrought of crystals; and white banners broke and fluttered from the battlements in the morning breeze, and high and far he heard a clear ringing of silver trumpets.[94]

Tolkien saturates his readers with sights, sounds, colors, sensory impressions. The luxury of "pearl," silver," "crystals," and the courtly nature of "banners," "trumpets," "towers"—these all paint a picture for readers of a place of regal majesty. Tolkien proclaims it "tall and fair and shapely," suggesting that it, like Rivendell, has enough aesthetic beauty to summon a cry from Pippin. This is a structure that mimics the color and awe of the natural world; unlike Isengard, which is a place of death and brutality, Minas Tirith shows the power of humanity to create beautiful structures that enhance the viewers' appreciation of the environment.

Another place of environmental beauty in Minas Tirith is the Houses of Healing. In this place, healing is not only a medical practice. Instead, it is a holistic relationship between nature and people. Healing here is augmented by gardens and a kinship with nature. Tolkien is suggesting, therefore, that nature is integral to the characters' holistic well-being. They cannot be whole and healthy without connecting to their environments, just as the novels imply readers cannot be spiritually whole and healthy without an apprehension of and care for their natural world. Legolas adds his perspective on what Minas Tirith, just the site of an intense and violent battle, needs: "'They need more gardens. . . . The houses are dead, and there is too little here that grows and is glad. If Aragorn comes into his own, the people of the Wood shall bring him birds that sing and trees that do not die.'"[95] The Elf's first concern is to fill the city with life of a different kind—gardens, birds, and trees. Readers could dismiss his impulse as trivial when compared to the death and destruction that has just occurred, but Legolas's sincerity must make us pause. Through fantastic recovery, we see his desire as a legitimate one: life and gladness are not inconsequential; instead, they are necessary parts of our human existence, and here Tolkien is showing one way we find them—kinship with our natural world.

Through all these descriptions, readers can appreciate how nature, whether alone or inhabited, has the potential to be beautiful, powerful, even dangerous, yet always worthy of our attention, respect, and care. Other natural spaces that have not been described here (Fanghorn Forest, Moria, Junction, and other cities on Arrakis, for example) show equally remarkable landscapes, each with its own unique characteristics and charms. Thus, while this chapter is not an exhaustive list of each place in the Legendarium and the Duniverse, readers can apply the same ecocritical activities to those other environments to gain insight into how the authors have created and appreciated a wealth of diverse natural spaces. However, the consequences of not showing proper care and respect for nature are evident in the next examples of environments that have been neglected and abused.

Isengard, Mordor, and Giedi Prime: Abused Nature

Tolkien's and Herbert's landscape descriptions encompass many different kinds of natural spaces, ranging from the familiar and charming to the strange and even ugly. In their mythopoeic stories, the authors' maleficent characters tend to be aligned with uglier landscapes, usually as a result of having created or contributed to such ugliness. In these cases, the environments are to be despised or pitied, not because of their inherent ugliness, but because they have become the victims of flawed ethical systems. Thus, the emotional reactions our characters (or we) have to them are not necessarily the same as what they have to wild, untamed, or even dangerous places we encounter elsewhere—these landscapes have little redeeming value because they are under the purview of corrupted beings. And often, they are beyond redemption—a sobering fact and one that reinforces an ecocritical principle from earlier—that nature *is* real and has real consequences. Some of the physical consequences of such reckless interference are detailed in Isengard and Moria in Middle-earth and Giedi Prime in the Duniverse.

One of perhaps the saddest landscapes in *The Two Towers*, Isengard clearly shows the devastating results of careless industrialization, dehumanization, and greed on both the environment and on its inhabitants. As Aragorn and the men of Rohan ride toward Saruman's tower, they can see the changes to the landscape from its former state,[96] especially how the local resources have been affected by abuse: "The riders looked down upon the crossings, and it seemed strange to them; for the Fords had ever been a place full of the rush and chatter of water upon stones; but now they were silent. The beds of the stream were almost dry, a bare waste of shingles and grey sand."[97] Not only does this passage describe what the riders see on a literal, descriptive level, but it suggests again an anthropomorphic presence to nature. The Fords' "rush and chatter" have been silenced, almost like the voices of nature being quieted. The "almost dry" stream beds take on an empty, lonely quality without the joyful noise of their former selves. Tolkien continues to underscore the contrast between what was and what now is; such emphasis reinforces the drama of these scenes, but it also suggests that readers should mourn along with the characters for how these abuses have robbed the land of its former beauty. As chapter 3 will explore, time is a theme in both authors' works: it is limited, so the characters must work to use it wisely but also to respect and preserve what they can of the past. One of the ways that Tolkien illustrates this theme is through descriptions of landscapes as they now are contrasted with what they once were: "The air above was heavy with fog, and a reek lay on the land about them. . . . Once [the valley] had been fair and green, and through it the Isen flowed, already deep and strong . . . and all about it there had lain a pleasant, fertile land."[98] Tolkien engages readers' senses with the sight of heavy fog, the smell of the land's "reek," playing against the images of "fair," "green," "deep," "strong," "pleasant," and "fertile." In essence, Tolkien is using a language of rot and decay against one of new life and growth (a language that finds its zenith in Mordor).

Some of the most upsetting descriptions follow, relentless in their depiction of devastation and revelatory of Saruman's true personality: "Beneath the walls of Isengard there still were acres tilled by the slaves of Saruman; but most of the valley had become a wilderness of weeds and thorns. Brambles trailed upon the ground, or clambering over bus and bank, made shaggy caves where small beasts housed. No trees grew there; but among the rank grasses could still be seen the burned and axe-hewn stumps of ancient groves."[99] Here, Tolkien's language leaves little doubt as to the remorse readers should feel when encountering this land. The land is like a twisted reflection of the Shire: instead of Hobbits tilling the land, it is Saruman's "slaves"; the result is not the rich green fields of Hobbiton but instead a "wilderness of weeds and thorns." Where the Hobbits dwell in their comfortable Hobbit holes, "small beasts" inhabit "shaggy caves" made of "brambles." And, tragically, the dead remains of trees remind readers of their prematurely shortened lives, "burned" and "axe-hewn stumps"—the language is almost evocative of a battlefield. As the travelers arrive at Saruman's doorstep, readers see death and darkness depicted in even more demoralizing detail:

> Shafts were driven deep into the ground; their upper ends were covered by low mounds and domes of stone, so that in the moonlight the Ring of Isengard looked like a graveyard of unquiet dead. For the ground trembled. The shafts ran down by many slopes and spiral stairs to caverns far under; there Saruman had treasuries, store-houses, armouries, smithies, and great furnaces. Iron wheels revolved there endlessly, and hammers thudded. At night plumes of vapour steamed from the vents, lit from beneath with red light, or blue, or venomous green.[100]

The "graveyard of unquiet dead" and the "venomous" vapors leave little doubt in the readers' minds that this land is unwell. Saruman's abuse stems largely from his desire to industrialize, to add to his "treasuries, store-houses, armouries, smithies, and great furnaces." His greed and exploitation have poisoned the once fair land, and Tolkien does not allow either Saruman or his readers to misinterpret the horror of what has been done.

On their way to destroy the One Ring, Sam and Frodo encounter many horrible landscapes. The Dead Marshes foreshadow some of the experiences to come in Mordor: "Cold clammy winter still held sway in this forsaken country. The only green was the scum of livid weed on the dark greasy surfaces of the sullen waters. Dead grasses and rotting reeds loomed up in the mists like ragged shadows of long-forgotten summers."[101] The marshes house some forms of life in their weeds, though it is mostly rotten and decaying life, life that is in the process of ceasing; they give the reminder of "long-forgotten summers" and the growth that must have flourished then. However, this is a space that has been overtaken by death: it was the site of an ancient battlefield that over time consumed all the fallen dead and became the toxic marshlands at the time of the War of the Ring. Tolkien implies that violence against people can have consequences on the land, too—that violence frequently leads to the degradation of all that surrounds it.

Mordor certainly illustrates this idea of the destructive capability of violence on nature; the home of the most powerful and evil creature in Middle-earth, Mount Doom's landscape is, if possible, more evocative of death and torture than any other place in the Legendarium. As in *The Two Towers,* Tolkien does not allow his readers to escape from the palpable wastelands of Mordor. We find pages upon pages of desolation, ugliness, and evil. Tolkien forces his readers to confront a dramatized result of environmental and moral damage.[102] Readers cannot avoid the imagery of Mordor, and it is exhausting: "Hard and cruel and bitter was the land that met [Sam's] gaze . . . there rose another ridge, much lower, its edge notched and jagged with crags like fangs that stood out black against the red light behind them . . . In such an hour of labour Sam beheld Mount Doom, and the light of it . . . now glared against the dark rock faces, so that they seemed to be drenched with blood."[103] Unlike the beauty of Minas Tirith, Mount Doom is "black" and "red," its heights marked by "notched and jagged" "fangs" seemingly "drenched with blood." The contrast in these two places' imagery is stark. Later, Tolkien describes some of the vegetation that survives (though how it does so mystifies both Sam and readers); his word choice is at odds with the notion of growing plants: "Dying," "harsh, twisted, bitter, struggling for life"; "long stabbing thorns"; "hooked barbs that rent like knives"; "maggot-ridden buds."[104] Mount Doom is no better, with "its feet founded in ashen ruin, its huge cone rising to a great height, where its reeking head was swathed in cloud. . . . [A] hateful land; all seemed ruinous and dead, a desert burned and choked."[105] While Isengard and even the Dead Marshes have the vestiges of past life in them,[106] Mordor is utterly wasted, perhaps beyond repair. The exhaustion and despair Frodo and Sam must overcome is immersive—emotional, psychological, and environmental. If readers are moved by these passages, they can make the connection between the Secondary World's environmental degradation and their own Primary World's; like Mordor, our land's resources are finite. Once their limits are reached, we will be encountering a spent land, not as horrific as Mount Doom perhaps, but equally as tragic. We might look to how to correct our relationship with our own ecosystems by reexamining our attitudes toward and treatment of nature.

In the Duniverse, one of the places also harmed by careless industrialization and squandering of resources is Giedi Prime, the home of the dishonorable House Harkonnen. This planet is an industrial wasteland, relying on mining, factories, and industrial manufacturing to support its economy. As a result, Giedi Prime's ecosystem has been poisoned by industrial pollution. In *Dune*, readers see evidence of slavery, gladiator-style games, and class-wide combat training. Giedi Prime's society is based upon the acquisition of power, and the Harkonnens typify the pursuit of power at any cost. Even thousands of years later, the Harkonnens' environmental devastation is still apparent. As one of the Atreides' descendants, Teg, travels through Giedi Prime (renamed Gammu), there is evidence of slow improvements to the planet's environment, yet it is still a place of ugliness, especially in the cities:

> They were well into Ysai and he glimpsed the black bulk of the ancient Harkonnen seat of Barony.... The car turned onto a street of small commercial establishments: cheap buildings constructed for the most part of salvaged materials that displayed their origins in poor fits and unmatched colors. Gaudy signs advised that the wares inside were the finest, the repair services better than those elsewhere. It was not that Ysai had deteriorated or even gone to seed, Teg thought. Growth here had been diverted into something worse than ugly. Someone had chosen to make this place repellent. That was the key to most of what he saw in the city."[107]

Unlike the well-ordered nature on Chapterhouse, or even the desolate beauty of Arrakis, Giedi Prime remains an abused ecosystem, one that has been made deliberately "repellent." Instead of stepping-stones amid fruit trees and buzzing bees, readers are faced with "cheap buildings" of "unmatched colors" and "gaudy signs," creating an effect that is "worse than ugly." Even outside of the urban centers, this planet offers little untainted nature: "[Lucilla] did not feel lucky as she looked out the second story window of this isolated Gammu farmhouse. The window was open and an afternoon breeze carried the inevitable smell of oil, something dirty in the smoke of a fire out there. The Harkonnens had left their oily mark on this planet so deep it might never be removed."[108] The descriptions of Gammu hearken back to Tolkien's of Isengard and Mordor—places that have not simply been abandoned but instead are the victims of an active, malicious hand in their degradation. All these places suggest there may be a permanence to this degradation; Mount Doom is a "hateful land," totally devastated by Sauron, while the Harkonnens "had left their oily mark" on Gammu so completely that the pollution might not be reversed. These sobering details suggest to readers that nature will not always remain as the source of beauty and comfort that they encountered in other chapters; instead, it can be harmed beyond repair, and thus the conscientious reader must look to himself or herself to ensure that individual responsibility is taken for enhancing our understanding of nature as something to be cared for and protected, not used for our own conveniences.

However, to end this chapter on a note of hope and healing, Tolkien does not let us forget that nature exists and persists, even in the face of evil and destruction: "There, peeping among the cloud-wrack above a dark tor high up in the mountains, Sam saw a white star twinkle for a while. The beauty of it smote his heart, as he looked up out of the forsaken land, and hope returned to him. For like a shaft, clear and cold, the thought pierced him that in the end the Shadow was only a small and passing thing: there was light and high beauty for ever beyond its reach."[109] The star Sam sees elicits both an emotional and an intellectual (even spiritual) reaction. He feels the beauty of the star, renewing his sense of hope, but he has a profounder realization—that evil ("the Shadow") is transient in the face of nature's wonder. The "light and high beauty" will endure untouched, uncorrupted forever, much like goodness itself.[110] Here again Tolkien interlocks morality and the environment—nature (or at least what it represents: life, fertility, health, beauty, growth) and goodness are transcendent things that readers can look to for emotional and spiritual fulfillment. This is not to ignore or erase the reality of environmental devastation explored above; rather it is to remind readers to find inspiration in the value and diversity of human and nonhuman life. Perhaps we can transcend our present circumstances through communion with our ecosystems because these systems have something of the divine in them. Moreover, we might also be inspired to take action to protect and preserve the beauty of our natural spaces, as many of the characters in these mythopoeic fantasy texts do and which the next chapter will explore.

CHAPTER 3

HALFLINGS AND HARKONNENS

*How Middle-earth and Dune's Communities
Model Environmentalism*

According to ecocritical scholar William Howarth, an eco-critic is "'a person who judges the merits and faults of writings that depict the effects of culture upon nature, with a view toward celebrating nature, berating its despoilers, and reversing their harm through political action.'"[1] The last chapter examined how both Tolkien's and Herbert's mythopoeic fantasies portray an extraordinary variety of landscapes in such detail as to encourage a "celebration" of nature; the authors' depictions frame nature to be as important as the characters that inhabit the stories, worthy of respect and protection (an ecocritical and geocritical tenant). This chapter focuses more specifically on how the various communities in the Legendarium and the Duniverse relate to their environments, and how these relationships suggest either healthful or harmful models of environmental care. By positioning their heroes or morally "good" characters in a close, positive relationship with the land, both authors suggest that there is something as morally praiseworthy in caring for this land as there is in their characters' other moral actions; the villainous characters' blatant disregard for the land and its protection implies a callous, cavalier attitude that readers should best avoid. Through these examples of culture (the different communities) affecting nature, readers see that the authors generally "berate" nature's "despoilers" while encouraging a "reversal of harm," where possible.

As chapter 2 acknowledged, Matthew Dickerson and Jonathan Evans's *Ents, Elves, and Eriador: The Environmental Vision of J. R. R. Tolkien* and Susan

Jeffers's *Arda Inhabited: Environmental Relationships in* The Lord of the Rings each addresses the interactions between Tolkien's characters and their environments, and they group these interactions as either positive or negative in their impact on the Middle-earth landscapes. For example, Jeffers theorizes that Ents, Hobbits, and Elves have the most egalitarian relationship with their environments by having "power with" the land and thus operating based upon "community"; Dwarves and Men draw "power from" the land, maintaining a certain distance from it but not necessarily harming it via "dialectic" (Hegel's theory describing the apprehension of a thing by defining it in opposition to another thing—Self as defined by Other, for example);[2] finally, Sauron, Saruman, and the Orcs take "power over" their lands, obviously enacting the most negative and harmful relationship with their environments because of the dynamic of "oppression" upon which this model operates.

Dickerson and Evans categorize various groups in terms of such environmental labels as stewardship, agrarianism, conservation, and horticulture, to name a few. While I will utilize some of the significant language used by these scholars, this chapter's purpose is to show more general categorizations of healthful/harmful ecological relationships; what is more significant is how both Tolkien and Herbert place connections between the human and nonhuman worlds in a moral framework. As Jeffers notes, "In *The Lord of the Rings*" (and in the Duniverse, I would add), "the decision to act in harmony with one's environment is a moral imperative."[3] While both Middle-earth and Dune are "fallen places" and "therefore no group can be said to act perfectly in relation to the environment," the actions these characters take emphasize the "tension . . . between imperfection and redeemability or grace."[4] As chapter 2 was not an exhaustive list of all the different landscape descriptions in the Legendarium and the Duniverse, this chapter cannot encompass all the communities and their environmental choices. Instead, a few broad patterns will be evaluated: those groups that actively support and preserve their ecosystems, and those that harm and exploit their environments. Finally, Dickerson, Evans, and Jeffers all recognize that Tolkien's worldview makes space for the spiritual in addition to the human/biological. Herbert's writings, too, portray his human characters as striving for and achieving greatness beyond their human capabilities, suggesting a spiritual dimension to their lives. Thus, as this chapter again applies an ecocritical approach to analyzing these mythopoeic fantasy texts, I adopt this wider approach as the "acceptance of the presence of spiritual life in the nonhuman category offers a helpful addition to reading texts from an ecocritical perspective"[5] and can encourage readers to better serve the needs of humanity and our home.

Healthy Environmental Relationships

HOBBITS AND ATREIDES

Chapter 2 of this study reviewed how Tolkien has established a link between Hobbits and land in general, especially their home, the Shire. Whether through their attachment to that home or their desire to experience new places (largely through Bilbo and Frodo, as most Hobbits are not the adventuring types), Hobbits clearly care for and about their environments. Within the prologue, Tolkien gives readers a few important details to define their view of Hobbits: "Hobbits are an unobtrusive but very ancient people, more numerous formerly than they are today; for they love peace and quiet and good tilled earth: a well-ordered and well-farmed countryside was their favourite haunt. They do not and did not understand or like machines more complicated than a forge-bellows, a water-mill, or a hand-loom, though they were skillful with tools. . . . [They have] a close friendship with the earth."[6] Tolkien imbues Hobbits with many charming characteristics, and in some ways, as scholars and readers alike have noticed, they are more relatable to readers as a race than Men: more human in their simple pleasures and obvious shortcomings. Yet, an important detail in Tolkien's conception of this race is their "friendship" with the land, their desire for "good tilled earth" no less than "peace and quiet." They are a simple people, but not simplistic. In the above passage, Tolkien also sets up a dichotomy that will carry through this trilogy—that of advanced technology and its dangerous potential. The Hobbits, readers' first models of conscientious living, eschew advanced machinery. While Tolkien is not deliberately telling his audience to fear all such technology, there is the implicit suggestion that too much technology can take on a power of its own, threatening the quality of life the Hobbits have worked to achieve: "In fact, [the Hobbits] are willing to sacrifice short-term personal convenience for greater long-term good. . . . [A]lthough the Hobbits love comfort, they are not willing to use artificial interventions to secure comfort if doing so will endanger the environment in the long term."[7] The industry and hard work the Hobbits embrace is uncomplicated by cutting-edge innovations, whatever those might look like in Middle-earth; much like science fiction, works often picture the disconnect that technology can create between ourselves and our lived experiences (especially if technology does the work of living for us). Tolkien's Hobbits offer readers a vision of the benefits of "old-fashioned" hard work, engaged in directly and through a literal closeness with the land. As Jeffers observes, the Hobbits' bare feet characterize them as "very viscerally connected to their place . . . [a] humble, agrarian community."[8] Further, "the work they put in to the cultivation of their place makes them personally interested in its continuing growth,"[9] and the community's concern with the Shire derives from "a deep love for their home, a love that is rooted in a relationship with the Earth."[10] Patrick Curry notes, "The bucolic hobbits . . . fall within the long tradition in English letters of nostalgic pastoralism, celebrating a time 'when there was less noise and more green.'"[11]

However, Tolkien's pastoral vision has led some of his critics to judge this characterization of Hobbits as *too* bucolic and nostalgic.[12] Dickerson and Evans lay out some of the criticisms by environmental studies scholars of the agrarian idealism represented by the Shire and the Hobbits: "Norman Wirzba has written: 'It is dangerous to romanticize local community life, especially when we remember that local communities have often been susceptible to various forms of provincialism. Farming communities, for instance, have not always been respectful of the contributions of women, nor have they been very welcoming of foreigners or people with new ideas.'"[13] According to Brian Donahue, "'Most suburbanites . . . want to live within a quaintly farmed landscape, but few want to be farmers.'"[14] Nevertheless, Dickerson and Evans argue (with evidence from other scholars as support) such idealizing can serve as "imaginative inspiration"[15] for readers to discover a formerly held approach to right relations with the Earth. They also contend that Tolkien's depiction of the very shortcomings Wirzba identified (some Hobbits' narrow-minded provincialism and even class snobbery against farmers) suggests an implicit critique of such "romanticize[d] local community life." One could argue the Hobbits' relationship with nature even subverts such concerns—as readers, we might not decide to dig into a pile of manure and become farmers after reading *The Lord of the Rings*, but we can observe the cost (in community security, physical labor, and even lives) that the Hobbits must invest in their land. In short, if readers were given a story of Hobbits leading their idyllic lives without danger, trials, or change, then perhaps these critics would be justified. It is only through the entire trilogy's framework that readers can understand the individual pieces of Tolkien's environmental worldview, of which the Hobbits are an integral part. The author, too, did not intend the Hobbits to represent a perfect community: "Tolkien himself pointed out that 'hobbits are not a Utopian vision, or recommended as an ideal in their own or any age. They, as all peoples and their situations, are an historical accident—as the Elves point out to Frodo—and an impermanent one in the long view.'"[16] As readers will see, the Hobbits themselves become aware of their own impermanence over the course of their journey.

Another trait the Hobbits in these stories exhibit is a natural curiosity, including about new environments. Even if they are at first reluctant to be outside their own lands, Hobbits seem to appreciate new places for their variety and unique features. For example, Bilbo tells Gandalf he wants to "'see the wild country again before I die, and the Mountains,'"[17] while Frodo is "'still in love with the Shire, with woods and fields and little rivers.'"[18] While a brief exchange, this dialogue suggests to readers early on that there is a variety of environments in Middle-earth, even within Hobbiton and the Shire, and that there is room for an appreciation of each (also reinforcing the claims explored in the previous chapter). In other words, Tolkien does not automatically privilege one place over another, just as he does not privilege one race over another. Each land and race has a value and beauty of its own, emphasized through Tolkien's thorough descriptions. Curry picks up this discussion in terms of criticisms leveled at Tolkien's writings as perhaps being ethnocentric or even racist. Curry instead interprets the diversity of the land and the people as counter to this critique: "It is also striking that the races in Middle-earth are most striking in their variety and autonomy. I suppose that this *could* be seen as an unhealthy emphasis on 'race'; it seems to me rather an assertion of the wonder of multicultural difference. And given that most of Middle-earth's peoples are closely tied to a particular geography and ecology, and manage to live there without exploiting it to the point of destruction, isn't this what is nowadays called bioregionalism?"[19] Tolkien's landscapes and inhabitants showcase a variety of diverse life-forms, contributing to the fantasy's world-building but also affirming the "wonder of multicultural difference." Similarly, the Hobbits' journey through these different geographies and ecologies allows them to grow their worldview and appreciate the joys of these different environments, encouraging readers to adopt this perspective as well.

As laid out in chapter 1, Tolkien frequently encourages readers to "re-gain" a vision of nature as beautiful, valuable for its own sake, and worth protecting. The characters' reactions invite readers to apprehend the world of Middle-earth as a place of beauty and wonder. The Hobbits' initial journey through the borders of the Shire, for example, paint a picture of a beautiful, serene world. Their first encounter with Elves is marked by blazing stars, murmuring rivers, and general beauty, especially in "green" places: "Suddenly they came out of the shadow of the trees, and before them lay a wide space of grass.... There the green floor ran on into the woods, and formed a wide space like a hall, roofed by the boughs of trees."[20] Their surroundings are all seemingly benevolent and full of wonderful surprises. As they continue their travels, though, both Hobbits and readers gain a new sense of the scope of their world: it houses and affects much more than just these small people. Gildor, one of the Elves, reminds Frodo of this when the Hobbit says, "'I did not expect to meet [danger] in our own Shire.'"[21] Gildor remarks that places are not truly "owned" by their inhabitants, perhaps a hint of Tolkien's portrayal of stewardship and caretaking that becomes so central to the novels, both in terms of land and people: "'But it is not your own Shire.... Others dwelt here before hobbits were; and others will dwell here again when hobbits are no more. The wide world is all about you: you can fence yourselves in, but you cannot for ever fence it out.'"[22] Here, Gildor is specifically referencing the danger of evil beings such as the Ringwraiths, but readers can interpret his warning more broadly—the beauty and safety of the Shire are not exempt from the damage wrought by selfishness and greed, and neither are the Hobbits exempt from their responsibility to secure a safe, environmentally sustainable future for themselves and for others.[23] With this lurking threat of danger, Tolkien adds dramatic tension to his narrative, but its "real-life" message resonates with our current ecological crisis. Our own ecosystems face challenges of resource depletion, widening deserts, and shrinking biodiversity. Like the Hobbits, others will take up our places after us, and we should not simply choose to "fence out" these issues in the false belief that they will therefore disappear. Through Frodo and Gildor's conversation, Tolkien implies the dangers of such an insular worldview. Fortunately, though, the Hobbits gain a wider perspective through their travels: they recognize the interconnected nature of Middle-earth, of both ecosystems and inhabitants.

Frodo and Gildor's conversation also reinforces a feeling of myth-making, which calls to mind Tolkien's three functions of fantasy referenced in chapter 1. Gildor tells us that the Shire has a history, indeed a pre-Hobbit history, which will continue beyond the Hobbits' own existence. This sense of mythology and the passage of time pervades the trilogy and *The Silmarillion* and has important connections to environmentalism. To fulfill his three functions, Tolkien must make his fantasy a new vision of something already known (recovery), a way of seeing a potentially better world (escape), and a renewal of wonder in his readers (consolation). Including nature as a distinctive, vital part of his myth-making is one way he accomplishes these three functions, as can be seen in descriptions of the Shire and elsewhere throughout the novels. In short, if a love of environment and a desire to preserve nature are important in these stories, then Tolkien's linking of nature and myth gives nature a long and weighty history, thus placing a greater narrative emphasis on it and a greater responsibility for both characters and readers. Overall, Tolkien's depiction of the Hobbits implies that responsible agriculture is both admirable and necessary for the continued health of the Shire: "Tolkien offers us a vision of the complex interdependence of people, community, and land comparable to modern environmentalists' recognition that healthy human culture requires responsible agricultural use of the land.... The idea informing both modern thinking on the subject and Tolkien's perspective, exemplified in the Shire, is that of *sustainable agriculture*, which Tolkien portrays as an implicit concern in the societal mores of the people who live there."[24] Thus, we might dub the Hobbits sustainable agriculturalists or conservationists, holding "power with" the land in utilizing its resources responsibly and in a manner that will not exhaust them. As Jeffers asserts, "Tolkien offers a model—to readers, to ecocriticism, to humans generally—in which a place and its inhabitants connect in mutually beneficial ways, in which neither the human (extra-textually speaking) nor the land have to claim dominance to gain validity."[25] Such a lifestyle implies a healthful longevity in this ecosystem, one enriched by a close personal connection to the land and to its inhabitants.

The Atreides family represents such conservationists, too, even though their relationship to their environment shifts over the course of the novels. In the first novel, Herbert creates an immediate link between Paul and the land. Among his retinue from Caladan, Paul is the only character truly equipped to adapt to his new surroundings, and perhaps the only one who accepts Arrakis without serious reservation. As Tolkien does with the Hobbits, Herbert introduces Paul by positioning him within a natural place; in fact, the very first words of *Dune* emphasize the significance of environment and identity: "A beginning is the time for taking the most delicate care that the balances are correct. This every sister of the Bene Gesserit knows. To begin your study of the life of Maud'Dib, then, take care that you first place him in his time...

[a]nd take the most special care that you locate Maud'Dib in his place: the planet Arrakis. Do not be deceived by the fact that he was born on Caladan and lived his first fifteen years there. Arrakis, the planet known as Dune, is forever his place.[26] Like the Hobbits, Paul is defined by his environment. The land itself shapes him, albeit in a different way than how the Shire shapes the Hobbits.[27] Readers will see how the desert becomes a kind of testing ground for Paul, and it is his reactions to these tests that clearly underscore his environmental capabilities and, perhaps subtly, Herbert's environmental vision. Timothy O'Reilly observes the inextricable connection between Paul's heroism and his ecological awareness. For O'Reilly, Paul's prescient visions (partly Paul's unique ability, partly the result of spice-induced side effects) are essential to his ecological role in *Dune*:

> In a sense, what Herbert does in Paul's visions is to take ecological concepts to a much deeper level. Paul comes to see opposition between the aims of civilization and those of nature, as represented by the human unconscious. An ecosystem is stable not because it is secure and protected, but because it contains enough diversity that certain organisms will survive despite drastic changes in the environment and other adverse conditions. Strength lies in adaptability, not fixity. Civilization, however, tries to create and maintain security, which all too frequently crystallizes into an effort to minimize diversity and stop change.[28]

Perhaps differently from Tolkien, Herbert and modern environmental critics see "security" and "protection" as anathema to an ecosystem's health and "strength," and so those like Wirzba and Donahue could be justified in warning against the idyllic agrarianism of the Shire, seemingly stuck in "fix[ed]" and safe conditions. And yet, the Hobbits do experience the consequences of such "opposition between the aims of civilization and those of nature," particularly in the closing chapters detailing the scouring and rousing of the Shire. On a small scale, the Shire does diversify and "adapt" to the changing times of Middle-earth. After "Sharkey" industrializes much of the Shire, the Hobbits cannot live the same, isolated lives to which they have become accustomed. The corruption and destruction the Fellowship have faced in other parts of Middle-earth have not spared the Shire, and the Hobbits' task of purging Sharkey's forces and rebuilding their home necessitates a changed perspective, an environmental activism that displays this community's "adaptability." Thus, like Herbert's fiction, Tolkien's legendarium does take an environmental vision to the "deeper levels" O'Reilly identifies. And for readers of *Dune,* O'Reilly strikes on something integral: Paul both recognizes and embodies the numerous complexities that struggle throughout Herbert's chronicles. Paul must balance the needs of ecology with the needs of his leadership, the norms of civilization with the challenge of an untamed planet, as well as the "human unconscious" with which he is in contact through his web of visions. Herbert layers these complex elements in this first *Dune* novel, with Paul representing the environmental tensions presented to humanity on a consistent basis.

Nature works as a force impacting Paul's growth into an ecoconscious protagonist. Many of Herbert's epigraphs (like the one cited above) reveal how Paul's training has opened him up to an environmental sensitivity. For example, chapter 4's inscription catalogs the "wonderful companion-teachers" Paul had as his mentors.[29] He sees the beauty and potential of the land, appreciating its wildness (as the Fremen do) even though it is nothing like his home planet. As we saw in the previous chapter, much of the narrative is told through Paul's perceptions—how he encounters the planet, the people, the textures and smells and sounds. Through Paul, readers see the planet with this positive perspective—we identify with him and therefore reenvision what is before us through fantastic recovery. We see Arrakis not as a barren land without value but as an infinitely invaluable space—a home for Paul, for the Fremen, for a culture that values natural spaces and "berates" its "despoilers."[30] Like the Hobbits and, of course, the Fremen, Paul has "power with" the land, working alongside it to preserve its resources. Indeed, by the end of the first novel, Paul pledges to create a more fertile world: "'The Fremen have the word of Muad'Dib,' Paul said. 'There will be flowing water here open to the sky and green oases rich with good things. But we have the spice to think of, too. Thus, there will always be desert on Arrakis . . . and fierce winds, and trials to toughen a man. We Fremen have a saying: "God created Arrakis to train the faithful." One cannot go against the word of God.'"[31] While Paul's plan has unintended negative consequences, for the purposes of the first novel, Herbert highlights the nobility of Paul in taking up the planet's cause, balancing the planet's potential for a transformation "rich with good things" and the original desert. Paul improves what can be improved and preserves that which needs preserving, offering readers an example of a healthful environmental relationship that works with nature rather than destroying it.

TOM BOMBADIL, THE ENTS, AND THE FREMEN

Tom Bombadil offers readers another positive environmental role model.[32] He is separate from the happenings of Middle-earth, yet separate for an important and praiseworthy purpose. He is driven by his own motivations, underscoring how nature is something to be preserved for its own sake, over and above what it offers to humans, or in this case, what it offers to other races or species. Tom is another model for how to treat the world—he is "master," but not in an enslaving, dominating sense. Instead, he is a protector, ally, and advocate for nature. Goldberry explains this to the Hobbits, as they ask who he is: "'He is the master of wood, water, and hill.'" "'Then all this strange land belongs to him?'" "'No indeed! . . . The trees and the grasses and all things growing or living in the land belong each to themselves. Tom Bombadil is the Master.'"[33] Like his colleague C. S. Lewis, who felt the obligation of people to exercise humble authority over creation, Tolkien suggests that Bombadil is a master in the best sense. He does not control or own the land, much like Gildor said about the Hobbits and the Shire, but instead he protects it for its own sake, even Old Man Willow and the less peaceful creatures living there.[34] He allows each thing to "grow," "live," and thrive without dominating or using it for his own gain, a stark contrast with what we will find in *The Two Towers* and, indeed, with what we find in much of Herbert's writings. In fact, Liam Campbell positions Tom Bombadil as exhibiting traits that are in direct opposition to Saruman, each character respectively representing positive and negative models of environmental care and best understood via this contrast: "Tom Bombadil is not just 'the spirit of nature' but rather the embodiment of nature under threat,"[35] while "Saruman could be said most closely to resemble the real threat which Tolkien perceived was looming over the natural landscapes of the primary world: the emergence and seemingly unstoppable rise of industrialized power and the ever-growing potency of the machine."[36] More discussion of Saruman shortly, but let us turn back to Tom Bombadil.

As we saw in the last chapter, the Old Forest's beauty is ancient and dreamlike, while the areas that Tom Bombadil takes the Hobbits through have a more unreserved, joyful quality, similar perhaps to Tom Bombadil's and Goldberry's personalities. As the weary Hobbits come closer to Tom Bombadil's home, the landscape expresses some of that joy, as "they stepped out from the Forest, and found a wide sweep of grass welling up before them. The river, now small and swift, was leaping merrily down to meet them, glinting here and there in the light of the stars, which were already shining in the sky."[37] Here, the language evokes youth and lightness, contrasting distinctly from the heavy, plodding forest with its deep, slow river and ancient willows. Words such as "welling," "leaping merrily," "glinting" and "shining" create a much different mood, that of almost uncontrollable emotion and energy. The land changes even more as they come closer to Tom Bombadil's home, showing its alterations from the hands of its "owners": "The grass under their feet was smooth and short, as if it had been mown or shaven. The eaves of the Forest were clipped, and trim as a hedge. The path was now plain before them, well-tended and bordered with stone. It wound up on to the top of a grassy knoll, now grey under the pale starry night; and there, still high above them on a further slope, they saw the twinkling lights of a house."[38] Tom's influence over the land is evident: the grass seems "mown" rather than overgrown, the forest is as "trim as a hedge," the "well-tended and bordered" path leads to "twinkling lights." This place is orderly and inviting, similar to what the Hobbits are used to in the Shire. Yet, Tolkien seems to balance safe spaces with dangerous ones. Behind Tom's house, "the dark shapes of the Barrow-downs stalked away into the eastern night."[39] The author contrasts images of light and dark, order and wildness to describe Tom's home and the Barrow-downs. Ecocritics look for these concepts of balance; a healthful ecosystem has many kinds of life, and Middle-earth seems to demonstrate this principle as well. The Old Forest contains beauty and danger, as do Tom Bombadil's home and the Barrow-downs.[40] The trees in the Forest take on human-like qualities to draw attention to nature as a living, feeling part of our ecosystem; despite whatever negative qualities nature has (whether in this fictional story or in reality), it is deserving of our attention and care, just as beautiful or welcoming spaces are.

Perhaps the most important environmental presence in *The Two Towers*, Treebeard and the Ents have a deeply interconnected relationship to the land as they embody sentience but also exist as part of the landscape. They also have a special association with age, time, and memory (much like the Elves, as readers will see). Merry and Pippin's first encounter with Treebeard gives us this connection: "'One felt as if there was an enormous well behind [Treebeard's eyes], filled up with ages of memory and long, slow, steady thinking; but their surface was sparkling with the present; . . . it felt as if something that grew in the ground . . . had suddenly waked up, and was considering you with the same slow care that it had given to its own inside affairs for endless years.'"[41] Treebeard's "slow care" and "long, slow, steady thinking" typify his personality—Ents are deliberate in their decision-making and not easily hurried. However, Tolkien accomplishes something significant here: By characterizing Fanghorn (both the individual and the forest) in such a way, Tolkien encourages readers to make a connection between the qualities of his fictional forest and the value of real-life forests and green spaces. The forest has a mystery and power to it, the representation of this long, slow care that has been pondering itself and its world for ages. This lends a wondrous, valuable quality to Fanghorn and, through the act of recovery, to our own trees and forests. The implication is that if we abuse or destroy such spaces, we lose the beauty, the memories, the slow care that these places "house." Here we move beyond appreciating nature to perhaps a desire to protect and preserve nature.

Tolkien also connects Treebeard to Tom Bombadil. Like Tom, Treebeard is somewhat apart from the concerns of Men and Hobbits and other races. He states his position as such: "'I do not like worrying about the future. I am not altogether on anybody's *side,* because nobody is altogether on my *side* . . . ; nobody cares for the woods as I care for them.'"[42] Treebeard sees the mistreatment of trees and the environment that surrounds his home, and he asserts that it is important not only to protect his home but to *care* about it, to be emotionally moved. It is hard not to be moved by the sadness of Treebeard's words. He also raises the idea that people have an obligation to their neighbors, that they cannot be isolated forever: "'I used to be anxious when the shadow lay on Mirkwood, but when it removed to Mordor, I did not trouble for a while; Mordor is a long way away . . . But Saruman now! Saruman is a neighbor: I cannot overlook him. I must do something, I suppose.'"[43] Tolkien suggests here that while some of us can choose to distance ourselves from environmental carelessness, we have a duty to our neighbors. The implication is that, by extension, we are all neighbors, and destruction of one land can have far-reaching and sometimes irreversible consequences. Isengard's industrialization causes much of the detrimental consequences to Fanghorn, which in turn have their own far-reaching consequences.

The Fremen are similar to both the Hobbits and Ents in their relationship with the environment—there is a symbiotic quality to their existence on Arrakis, and they, too, are affected in complicated ways by the passage of time. In the first novel, they begin as very in-touch with their planet. They have been shaped by the desert, knowledgeable in its ways and how to survive. Their ambition (whether genuine or "implanted" by the Bene Gesserit or Liet-Kynes) is to transform their planet and create a more habitable and gratifying home. Like the Hobbits, we can understand the Fremen from a bioregional context. They work to enact "local" care (even if that label extends to a vast desert/desert planet), surviving as a people and sustaining their environments through careful awareness of and respect for their land.[44] Similar to Tolkien, Herbert ultimately portrays the delicate balance and interconnectedness of humans and nature: "because of irresponsible sovereign power [in Arrakis], bioregions are vulnerable to destruction-by-consumption; therefore the conditions of possibility for a future of any kind are precarious . . . [and] this vulnerability demands a responsible, democratic program of action insofar as bioregions are valuable as sites of possibility for capable and creative life and cultural integrity, not only as minimal conditions for bare life."[45] The "capable and creative life and cultural integrity" Anderson describes emerge through Paul's "liberation" of the Fremen from Harkonnen rule, Arrakis's terraforming, and (eventually) Leto II's "Golden Path."

Yet, as generations pass, the Fremen change, as outlined earlier. The planet makes them "softer" and more vulnerable, but they are also changed by a corrupt government, imperfect leaders, and the struggles of factions continually in conflict. Their relative isolation in the desert of *Dune* gives way to varied interactions between off-world travelers. By the time of Leto II in *God Emperor of Dune,* they lack the same integrity and moral codes of earlier years. Have they gained anything by this softening? How do they answer the challenge of their planet's environment? The *Dune* chronicles are, in many ways, stories about tests—spiritual, emotional, and intellectual tests. As Herbert's characters are challenged again and again over generations, their attitudes and decisions speak clearly about their morality, their unique perspectives, and their relationships with nature. In the first *Dune* novel, however, the Fremen represent one of the most healthful relationships with nature, having "power with" the land; even though they work to transform the desert into something lush, they refuse to do so at the expense of precious resources, whether human or nonhuman.

The Fremen present a communal lifestyle that lives in harmony with one another and with the desert. In fact, the desert and water are an integral part of their cultural rituals, lending a spiritual significance to these natural forces. For example, when one of the Atreides soldiers dies in the desert, the Fremen embrace the spiritual "bond" they share with him: "'We will treat your comrade with the same reverence we treat our own,'" the Fremen said. "'This is the bond of water. We know the rites. A man's flesh is his own; the water belongs to the tribe.'"[46] The Fremen honor and respect the individual person, but not above the needs of the tribe and the ecosystem, a holistic approach to life rather than an individualistic one. Herbert tells readers that the Fremen exercise a profound self-control, one that could encourage readers to see the value in patient, careful environmental stewardship like that enacted by the Fremen: "*The Fremen were supreme in that quality the ancients called 'spannungsbogen'—which is the self-imposed delay between desire for a thing and the act of reaching out to grasp that thing.*"[47] Unlike the Harkonnens or Saruman, for example, who "grasp" whatever they "desire" for their own gain, the Fremen interfere with their environments only when necessary for the health of themselves or for the environment itself.[48] When Jessica and Paul see some of the Fremen's water reclamation projects, Stilgar (a loyal Fremen tribal leader) explains the great amount of self-control the Fremen have: "Stilgar looked at her. 'There were those among us in need of water,' he said, 'yet they would come here and not touch this water. Do you know that?' . . . 'We have more than thirty-eight million decaliters here.' . . . 'A treasure trove,' she said."[49] Stilgar explains what this water means for their future as the scene takes on a religious ritualistic quality, with the Fremen chanting in their native language and Stilgar replying with their ecological plan, a kind of call-and-response:

> "We will trap the dunes beneath grass plantings. . . . We will tie the water into the soil with trees and undergrowth. . . . Each year the polar ice retreats. . . . We shall make a homeworld of Arrakis—with melting lenses at the poles, with lakes in the temperate zones, and only the deep desert for the maker and his spice. . . . And no man ever again shall want for water. It shall be his for dipping from well or pond or lake or canal. It shall run down through the qanats to feed our plants. It shall be there for any man to take it. It shall be his for holding out his hand."[50]

Jessica senses the "religious ritual" in what Stilgar and his tribe are saying and notices "her own instinctively awed response."[51] She concludes that this vision "was a dream to capture men's souls."[52] These descriptions invite readers to see our own interactions with nature as important as a religious ritual, more than just an ordinary process. This is one example of the sacralization of nature referenced in chapter 1—Tolkien and Herbert often show their characters confronted with nature in a moment of spiritual reflection, evoking similarly "awed responses" from these characters.

Another Fremen character who models positive environmental stewardship can be found in Liet-Kynes, and his passing marks an important chapter of the first novel: it gives an outside perspective to the larger environmental concerns facing humanity. This passage could be viewed as one of the author's most clear communications with his audience, one that incorporates both information specific to the novel but also ecological directives that can be received and applied on a general level to perceptive readers. As Kynes is left to die in the desert (a tragically ironic fate), Herbert simultaneously juxtaposes the enormity of nature and Kynes's apparent insignificance with Kynes's critical role in preserving this nature, thus suggesting Kynes's very significant role (and ours, too). In many ways, Kynes acts as a John the Baptist–type character, "preparing the way" for the messiah, Paul, who comes after him.[53] The chapter begins with Kynes as nameless ("The man crawled across a dunetop"),[54] perhaps highlighting his characterization as an Everyman. Nature is supreme, as Kynes is "a mote caught in the glare of the noon sun."[55] However, Kynes soon asserts his identity: "'I am Liet-Kynes,' he said, addressing himself to the empty horizon.... 'I am His Imperial Majesty's Planetologist,' he whispered, 'planetary ecologist for Arrakis. I am steward of this land.'"[56] Even in his doomed ending, Kynes attempts to make sense of his place within the universe, and in many ways he acts as Paul does throughout the novel. He has unerring confidence coupled with humanizing doubt. His title and identity are useless in death, and he soon recognizes this: "*I am steward of this sand.*"[57] His understandable cynicism is balanced by the memory of his father, perhaps a stand-in for Herbert himself and also a predictor of Paul's role on Arrakis. Unlike Paul, however, Kynes wants to close his ears to the words of his father, refusing to acknowledge that his role in the universe is part of a larger ecosystematical picture. Even when faced with a role on Dune that could lead to jihad, Paul does not close his mind to the needs of the planet, demonstrating acute environmental sensitivity.

Despite Kynes's unfortunate fate, his death still provides an essential understanding of the author's larger motives in writing *Dune*. The piece of environmental wisdom that Kynes's consciousness sifts through speaks most strongly of the importance of appreciating one's planet and all it provides. Herbert portrays the loyalty that Kynes feels towards his planet: "A thought spread across his mind—clear, distinct: *The real wealth of a planet is in its landscape, how we take part in that basic source of civilization—agriculture.* And he thought how strange it was that the mind, long fixed on a single track, could not get off that track.... *We don't die easily. I should be dead now ... I will be dead soon ... but I can't stop being an ecologist.*"[58] Much like Paul, Kynes cannot escape his destiny, whether it be through his identity as ecologist or his death "at the impersonal hands of his planet."[59] However, Herbert does more in this chapter than just draw comparisons between characters. The subconscious voice of Kynes's father tells readers just what ecology is and how it functions—on Arrakis, as a theme in the novel, and in reality. According to Kynes's father, "the highest function of ecology is understanding consequences."[60] The author has efficiently summarized diverse connotations of environment and polished them into one lucid concept: that consequences are at the root of all environmental concerns. Likewise, Paul recognizes (in large part because of his prescient visions) that there are inescapable consequences to every action, and therefore one's position in the universe is not to be taken inconsequentially. Kynes's father continues to build upon this concept of action-consequence, and through it he highlights an important perspective on the protagonist, Paul. The scene also lends a sense of urgency to our own world's environmental needs, especially the need for us to find better equilibrium in our own environments. As Brian Herbert explains, "Liet-Kynes is a metaphor for Western man, bearing all the adornments of scientific and cultural knowledge. But the rhythms of his life and Imperial society, like the rhythms of Western society, are out of synch with the rhythms of the planet."[61] Kynes is not entirely wrong in his attempts to change the planet's ecology, but he ultimately fails where Paul succeeds because Paul can find the "rhythms" of Dune. Ultimately, like the Hobbits, Tom Bombadil, and the Ents, the Atreides, Kynes, and the Fremen all underscore how pivotal healthy environmental relationships are, and their nobility as characters is directly tied to how they treat their ecosystems, further emphasizing how important such models of environmental stewardship should be for readers.

Other Healthy Relationships

THE ELVES, BENE GESSERIT, AND DWARVES

As the Hobbits journey throughout Middle-earth, they find themselves in various new environments, which Tolkien uses to show the rich variety of places in his imagined world, each with its own unique features and impact on the travelers. In Rivendell, Tolkien gives us a picture of a place marked by rest and healing. Like the Shire, it is described in idyllic terms, but it has its own distinct characteristics and functions. Tolkien provides numerous physical descriptions of Rivendell (a few of which can be found in the previous chapter), all tied to beauty, memory, and the passage of time, like the Elves themselves. While the Shire is more rustic, with an emphasis on gardening and agriculture, Elrond's home is a place for contemplation, remembrance of the past, and rest. In some ways, we could say it is more "upper-class"—the Elves are not concerned with physical labor or menial tasks. The beauty of Rivendell is more artificial perhaps than the Shire (though here "artificial" is not necessarily negative—it suggests artifice, and it also suggests a change from nature's original form). As we also saw in Lothlórien, the Elves are concerned with aesthetically pleasing spaces, and they have a love for workmanship and beauty, which Hobbits do not necessarily hold. Tolkien again shows readers a different model for how to interact with nature. Like the Elves, we can beautify our environments, synthesizing our own vision for what is attractive with what nature offers. The author does not suggest a superiority in Rivendell or the Elves' lands, just a different landscape and a different way of interacting with that landscape. Here, Tolkien's definition of "escape" comes to mind. We are not simply escaping our reality by reading about Rivendell, but we are being shown a version of what our own world could be, if we valued beauty and knowledge and rest in an increasingly busy and utilitarian world. Likewise, if we valued simplicity and "friendship with the land," we might have our own version of the Shire.

Herbert's portrayal of the Bene Gesserit provides a complicated environmental mode. While not actively harming their environments and, like the Elves, frequently beautifying their natural spaces, at times they do represent a disconnect between age and insight. They have had generations of "wisdom" and "training," which, while providing a basis for Paul's remarkable abilities, do not save them from falling victim to their own corruption and self-serving greed. Paul and his descendants consistently rebuke the Bene Gesserit for their twisted plots, their attempts to control genetic plans and create messiahs, to play "god" and manipulate others. Meanwhile, the Bene Gesserit are largely unconcerned with their ecosystems unless a threat to these ecosystems indicates a threat to their genetic plans. There appears an almost permanent division or boundary between the Bene Gesserit and genuine, intimate human and ecological interactions. They cannot lower their defenses enough to see past their dogma and schemes to care for their homes and value those spaces as more than a "breeding" ground to advance their dogma and genetic planning. While not as obviously immoral or corrupt as the Harkonnens, the Bene Gesserit suggest a certain separateness from their surroundings. This is a large part in why they are never as "successful" as the Atreides in creating long-lasting change, or of taking power.

For example, Herbert frequently presents external nature and how his characters respond to it (or not) as a way of defining their ecological sensitivities. In *Dune*'s first chapter, he underscores the Bene Gesserits' indifference to nature (unless, of course, it can present some benefit or advantage to them).[62] The "warm night at Castle Caladan" elicits no response from the Reverend Mother Gaius Helen Mohiam when she arrives and is escorted in the side door of the Castle.[63] In this chapter's next scene, the Reverend Mother awaits the approach of Paul and his mother Jessica: "Windows on each side of her overlooked the curving southern bend of the river and the green farmlands of the Atreides family holding, but the Reverend Mother ignored the view."[64] Whatever her reasons, she avoids nature's potential influence and places her "mission" of testing Paul to see if he has learned his lessons well above everything else around her. This scene suggests some irony—that the Reverend Mother herself has been tested by her surroundings and found lacking. Her apathy to her environment places certain blinders on her, a sightlessness that Paul does not experience. Paul's perpetual awareness of and response to his environment only reinforces his ecoconsciousness, particularly when contrasted with the seeming *lack* of awareness that other, more "experienced" persons (such as the Reverend Mother) exhibit. Jessica, too, could belong to this group of the "experienced."

If the Bene Gesserit do not have a completely healthy relationship with the land, Jessica disrupts this pattern, at least in part. Among the women in this holy order, Jessica aligns herself with and even begins to identify herself as Fremen,[65] yet this might only be through the Atreides' influence (and particularly through Paul's influence). She is affected by her environment, but she can never truly adapt to Arrakis; Caladan remains her true home, as she takes refuge in it in later years. Unlike Paul, she struggles to see the beauty and inherent value in the planet. It is quite possible that this attitude stems from the Bene Gesserit's influence on her—they, like most of the other communities in these books, see the planet as a tool. They have implanted prophecies and myths to serve their needs, and the ecology of Dune just helps to propel those messages. They do not value the land beyond its practical use, and thus, while fascinating and controversial characters, they fall short as truly effective models of a healthy relationship with their ecosystems.

While Jessica is remarkably similar to her son in her training and understanding, she, too, falls short of being a truly environmentally conscious figure (perhaps more akin to the communities that derive "power from" nature). She frequently demonstrates her ability to control conflicts and emotions with her "Voice," to exhibit feats of physicality similar to Paul, and even to predict situations she and her son will encounter. However, her preoccupation with the past and, therefore, her inability to completely *adapt* keep her from achieving the "greatness" and power that Paul does. From their very first days on Arrakis, Jessica cannot remove Caladan from her mind: "She shuddered, glanced at the slit windows high overhead. It was still early afternoon here, and in these latitudes the sky looked black and cold—so much darker than the warm blue of Caladan. A pang of homesickness throbbed through her. *So far away, Caladan.*"[66] Paul, however, finds no trouble in adapting to the planet. His eagerness to learn and be of service to his father outweighs his sentimentality. Paul cannot afford to live in his past but rather must look to his family's future.[67] Even after several years on the planet, inhabiting her role as Reverend Mother to the Fremen, Jessica does not have the same flexibility as Paul: "She knew she would never overcome a feeling of being in an alien place. It was the harshness that the rugs and hangings attempted to conceal."[68] For Paul's mother, the presence of the past and its unfinished possibilities can never leave her consciousness, cannot allow her to be a complete leader and ecological defender.

Jessica also lacks the total belief in Paul's identity as Fremen Lisan al-Gaib (or savior) that the other Fremen have, and at times she underestimates the Fremen's entire belief system. She sees only the superior presence of the Bene Gesserit in planting the "myths" that the Fremen come to hold. Jessica seems doubtful that Paul is a fulfillment of the Fremen beliefs, something Paul does not doubt. With their first encounter with the Fremen, Jessica makes it clear that she sees their superstitions as no more than products of her people's intervention: "Jessica sighed, thinking: *So, our Missionaria Protectiva even planted religious safety valves all through this hell hole. Ah, well . . . it'll help, and that's what it was meant to do . . . If only he knew the tricks we use!*"[69] In contrast, though he recognizes the hand of the Bene Gesserit, Paul is not as eager to dismiss the Fremen's belief in a savior as a carefully crafted farce; instead, he sees there are larger forces at work—the sandworms, the spice, the ecological plans—in shaping his destiny.

Jessica's motivation lacks the ultimate commitment to the planet Paul's has—she often makes her choices based upon her identity as mother and former partner of the Duke. Jessica sees only how something will benefit Paul, revealing her core identity as that of mother and "shield" to her son. After their first encounter with Stilgar's tribe, she is struck by the thought that the Fremen are *"an entire culture trained to military order. What a priceless thing is here for an outcast Duke!"*[70] She sometimes even reveals a kind of class superiority based on her status as Bene Gesserit and Leto's mistress, which Paul somehow avoids. Paul knows when to assert his authority as the Duke's son, but not to the denigration of the Fremen. Jessica, though awed by the Fremen, maintains a vestige of the kind of mindset that the Baron has: *"This is the scientist's dream ... and these simple people, these peasants, are filled with it."*[71] Jessica seems unable to separate a community's political status from its independent merits. The more Jessica becomes acquainted with Stilgar, the more admiration she feels, but she reveals a fixation with genetics: "*He has stature,* she thought. *Where did he learn such inner balance? ... What is his ancestry?* she wondered. *Whence comes such breeding?*"[72] These thoughts demonstrate how Jessica and, indeed, the Bene Gesserit cannot see past their breeding plans to a person's innate value. While Paul is certainly a product of such genetic planning and owes much of his success to that fact, he does not necessarily see "breeding" as the distinguishing feature of a person. He probes beyond simple characterizations of those around him, looking for a deeper, more complex nature of Arrakis and its inhabitants.

Moria is another example of Middle-earth's environmental diversity and, as Herbert does, Tolkien creates a more complex world by showing a people who are not necessarily the most healthful environmental role models. While not actively harming their lands, the Dwarves are like the Bene Gesserit— they use environments for personal gain. Nevertheless, Tolkien can turn this into a positive experience for readers—the Dwarves' homes are described with their own unique beauties. For Gimli, Moria is a place of remembered beauty[73]—a different beauty from the Shire or Rivendell, one with different appeals, primarily for its former greatness. Gimli tells Sam that the mines "'are not holes ... This is the great realm and city of the Dwarrowdelf. And of old it was not darksome, but full of light and splendor, as is still remembered in our songs.'"[74] Galadriel, too, shares her memory of Moria and its past beauty, impressing Gimli with her respectful descriptions. Tolkien shows readers how Moria has a complexity all its own—it obviously houses evil and greed, but it is also an example of how Dwarves have created their own environments. Like the Elves, they have used artifice to create their homes, but these places are also part of the natural world, an enhancement of it, in the Dwarves' opinions. The priceless Mithril imbedded in their rocks added beauty and value to the mines in the past, but it was also a cause of corruption and greed. Tolkien combines a few things here: there is a warning implicit in the Dwarves' fate—that desire for too much of a beautiful thing can be its own destruction. In addition, he gives us another example of recovery. By seeing Gimli's vision of Moria, readers can imagine the value of these mines and gain a new appreciation for somewhere they might not have otherwise viewed as beautiful or valuable. By pitting Elves and Dwarves against each other, Tolkien allows us to see both sides of their environments and environmental perspectives, and we can appreciate both.

Unhealthy Environmental Relationships

SARUMAN, SAURON, AND HARKONNENS

As the previous chapter explored, Isengard and Mordor are ravaged, unlivable lands, the result of greed and exploitation. The ugliness that is left in these lands is directly connected to the immorality of Saruman and Sauron. In addition, Tolkien repeatedly asserts an aesthetic focus—that beauty is important for its own sake, and something we should not be ashamed to value. Tolkien's writings imply that the moral intent behind our cultivation of beauty and of usefulness is most important. The Dwarves have their faults, as mentioned earlier, but they make things of both beauty and use. Saruman makes things of use, but for evil and ugliness. Within Tolkien's myths, there is not or should not be a place for ugliness—it is a reflection of the poor moral quality of the person behind it. Like Melkor in *The Silmarillion*, Saruman's sub-creation is misguided. By extension, we can feel an imperative to do that which is helpful but also beautiful and lovely, like the Shire and the Elves. Even the people of Rohan are sensitive to their lands' damage. They are not enacting some grand ecological scheme, but they are in touch with their animals and their environment.[75] Theoden notices the changes around him as they travel in Rohan and Isengard under the enemy's threat: "'They bring fire,' said Theoden, 'and they are burning as they come, rick, cot, and tree. This was a rich vale and had many homesteads. Alas for my folk!'"[76] While the Rohirrim are not as "courtly" as Gondor—more rustic and wild—Tolkien has given readers another example of a way of relating to their version of nature. They respect their horses, treating them as independent beings, and they value their fertile lands for how these places offer protection and a livelihood. Like Saruman, they value the use of things, but they have an attitude of respect and emotional engagement, unlike the White Wizard.

As the stories progress, readers are exposed to more and more ugly places. We have taken a quick glimpse into Isengard, and Frodo and Sam's journey with Gollum only brings us more depressing, polluted environments. The marshes, the stairs of Cirith Ungol, Shelob's lair, Mordor itself—these spaces show corruption, devastation, emptiness, desolation, and death. Tolkien employs language that fits the geography: "But always they found [the hills'] outward faces sheer, high and impassable, frowning over the plain below; beyond its tumbled skirts lay livid festering marshes where nothing moved."[77] "Frowning," "tumbled," "livid," "festering"—these descriptors reinforce the sad and awful results of a tarnished land. Tolkien emphasizes the real and immediate physical consequences of mistreating Middle-earth. As Frodo and Sam approach the Gates of Mordor,[78] which they won't be able to enter, they come closer to evil than they have been before, a place "defiled, diseased beyond all healing—unless the Great Sea should enter and wash it with oblivion. 'I feel sick,' said Sam. Frodo did not speak."[79] Tolkien continues with other unsavory details ("gaping pits," "poisonous mounds," "defiled" sunlight, "ash-heaps," "squeaking ghosts"); he is unrelenting in painting a picture of sadness and emptiness, and this picture literally sickens the Hobbits. It is hard not to feel moved by these images, and Sauron's pattern of destructive environmental choices should leave us motivated to ensure the same (albeit less epic in scale) destruction does not come to our homes and beloved places. And the land's condition is not some random, uncontrollable fate that had to happen to it (though in some sense, perhaps it did have to happen in order for redemption and healing to come). We can trace a direct line from *The Silmarillion* through the trilogy of all the pride, anger, and vengeance that have caused Elves, Men, and Dwarves to corrupt the beauty and function of Middle-earth, just as places of wonder and magnificence in our world that have been destroyed and abused are frequently the result of humanity's greed and domination.

Herbert, too, connects greed and domination to environmental degradation. The most obvious example of negative ecological role models in the first *Dune* novel is, of course, House Harkonnen. Readers are introduced to Baron Vladimir Harkonnen, his nephew Feyd-Routha, and his devious mentat, Piter, inside the dimly lit, suffocating confines of the Baron's chambers, covered in the trappings of his wealth and power. No acknowledgment or description of the physical features of his planet is offered to readers, and the setting of this room suggests something of the characters' values and attitudes. Their secrecy and manipulative machinations align with the atmosphere of this scene, and later details about the Harkonnens do not shine a better light on the family. If Paul derives power from building community with the Fremen, the Baron and his cohorts adopt the opposite approach. Herbert repeatedly uses these characters' language and dialogue to underscore their power-hungry ambitions, as the Baron's thoughts reveal: "*One must always keep the tools of statecraft sharp and ready. Power and fear—sharp and ready.*"[80] The weapon-like language of power as a "sharp" tool, always at the "ready," reveals a frightening mantra, one paired with the Baron's obsession with money, another source of the Baron's misguided power. The Baron counsels his equally power-hungry (albeit more stupid) nephew in the key to effective governance, which certainly does not include any considerations of environmental concern or sustainability: "The Baron sighed. 'I give you different instructions about Arrakis this time, Nephew. When last you ruled this place, I held you in strong rein. This time, I have only one requirement.' 'M'Lord?' 'Income.'"[81] While showing his utter greed and materialistic nature, the Baron has also revealed his lack of wisdom as a leader. He is willing to let go of all restraint on his dense and dangerous nephew to fully embrace a tyrannical reign for the sake of money. An alarming but unfortunately realistic consequence of this avarice is an abuse of people, a key resource in any ecosystem: "'Expensive, eh?' 'Expensive! . . . [S]queeze Arrakis for every cent it can give us. . . . Expensive,' the Baron sneered . . . 'Income then,' Rabban said. The Baron lowered his arm, made a fist. 'You must squeeze.' 'And I may do anything I wish as long as I squeeze?' 'Anything . . . [a]s long as you squeeze.'"[82] Herbert leaves no illusions about the Harkonnens' exploitative nature. The very words he chooses in this chapter denote violence and mistreatment of the planet and its people. On one level, readers could see this episode as an almost comical, exaggerated portrayal of villainous people and a villainous plot, highlighting by contrast Paul's ethical nature. However, a sobering fact is how relevant this exchange becomes when considered in light of our own environmental and political realities. We may not see all political or corporate leaders behind closed doors making fists and urging that their pawns "squeeze," but the results of selfish, materialistic, consumeristic decisions could not be clearer. The exploitations of Earth's own people and environmental resources continue to this day, over half a century after the publication of *Dune,* and the Baron's own greed is not so farfetched when viewed from our current vantage point.

    As Tolkien portrays how little the Hobbits are regarded as a serious force, the Fremen are continually underestimated as a force for change and power.

Perhaps one reason why the Baron has so little connection with his ecosystem is because he rarely leaves the interiors of any given location. He relies on the false support of his "suspensor" chair to move his body from place to place, crafting an artificially easy environment through which to both literally and figuratively maneuver himself. Therefore, to say he understands the way in which Arrakis operates, let alone the larger ecosystem of humanity of which he is a member, is quite an overstatement. As his conversation with Rabban draws to a close, he again reveals how little he understands (and, indeed, the Empire understands) the planet he hopes to abuse. Rabban, for all his dimness and naivety, comprehends that the Fremen represent a far greater threat than those in power would choose to recognize: "'It's difficult to count a population scattered among sinks and pans the way they are here. And when you consider the Fremen of—' 'The Fremen aren't worth considering!' 'M'Lord . . .' Rabban hesitated, frowning. 'I've always felt that we underestimated the Fremen, both in numbers and in—' 'Ignore them, boy! They're rabble.'"[83] In many ways, the Baron could be interpreted as a reflection of the common sentiment of superiority and oppression that class inequalities bring. The whole chapter is permeated with a stereotypical hierarchical mindset, that those without riches or power must be the victims of jealousy and unrest. The Baron confirms this, telling his nephew "'two things from Arrakis, then, Rabban: income and a merciless fist. You must show no mercy here. Think of these clods as what they are—slaves envious of their masters and waiting only the opportunity to rebel.'"[84] The Baron cannot see beyond the petty confines of greed and self-indulgence, willfully blinding himself to the necessary roles that all elements of an ecosystem play—instead, the Fremen (in many ways representative of various ethnic and cultural groups that have historically been marginalized) are merely something to be extorted along with their planetary resources. In strong contrast, Paul displays wisdom and compassion in harmonizing the efforts of the Fremen and the needs of the planet with his own leadership role. He does not initially assume power for its own sake, but for what he perceives (in conjunction with the Fremen's views, as well) to be the benefit of the planet, of the environment, of humanity. However, the Baron wants to turn Dune into a prison planet,[85] and even the Emperor deems the planet a "rat hole."[86] Paul sentences the Emperor to live on the Emperor's own prison planet, yet he shows a mercy so unlike the antagonists: "'But have no fear, Majesty. I will ease the harshness of the place with all the powers at my disposal. It shall become a garden world, full of gentle things.'"[87] These scenes not only provide a contrast in characters but heighten readers' awareness of how we should or should not interact with our environments, holding up a figurative mirror to our own choices and attitudes toward nature.

Another way readers can understand their own environmental choices is explored in *The Lord of the Rings* during the Council of Elrond. At this point in the novel, the characters need to decide what choices to make in the face of physical and environmental danger, and Gandalf voices what we might assume to be Tolkien's moral perspective: "'It is not our part here to take thought only of a season, or for a few lives of Men, or for a passing age of the world. We should seek a final end of this menace, even if we do not hope to make one.'"[88] This is a significant passage. According to Gandalf,[89] our duty is to goodness as a whole, not just to a part of it, such as protecting our own self-interest. Here is a message readers can take and use in their real lives, and one that they can apply to current human-driven environmental crises, if they choose to do so. If like the Hobbits we hope to preserve our own homes and safety and comfort, we have to look to the homes and safety and comfort of all—for the health and longevity of our ecosystems. This is not to place Tolkien inaccurately within a purely secular or environmentalist position or ignore the larger religious perspective from which the Inklings wrote, that people should look to things above, so to speak, and not to this world to satisfy desire. On the contrary, Tolkien's writings show how stewarding lands and loving environments are some of the ways to a better spiritual existence, one that refines our moral outlook and improves our treatment of each other. (In other words, by being good to the Earth, we are good to each other, and therefore embodying a moral imperative that most ecocritics would embrace). Religious and nonreligious readers alike can see the benefits of more positive relationships with the nonhuman world, relationships that can foster empathy, compassion, and humility as we find value in all of the world around us.

Alongside this message of ethical behavior, the above passage also asserts the importance of maintaining hope and not giving in to despair. This is something all of the Inklings maintained, and it set them apart as distinctive writers—maybe even distinctive mythopoeic writers. Their myths are not hopeless or purposeless but instead urge a pattern of ethical thought and behavior, regardless of results (in opposition to a utilitarian viewpoint that positions results and human benefits at the cost of environmental caretaking). Tolkien, Lewis, and Charles Williams especially seem to reject the pervasive Modernist notions of their times of futility and lack of purpose. Sam, for instance, repeatedly finds hope and optimism, even in the face of certain doom, death, starvation, and torture. In this sense, perhaps Sam is the truer hero of the novels; where Frodo despairs and falters, Sam perseveres with a quiet humility.[90] Sam has the bravery, like Bilbo, to do what needs to be done even when he feels scared, small, insignificant, and purposeless. He never abandons the trust that his actions can and will make a difference in the face of insurmountable difficulties and evil. If we want to extrapolate an environmental message in Sam's character, here we have one. Tolkien is encouraging us to take action, to look after others more than ourselves, and to trust that our contributions mean something in the larger world.

Nevertheless, for both Herbert and Tolkien, fate and choice are complicated and, at times, contentious forces. For example, as *The Two Towers* begins, we find an intersection between these two ideas. Several times in the opening chapters, Aragorn questions his choices and wonders what part he will play in the legend that he knows will follow these choices: "'And now may I make a right choice, and change the evil fate of this unhappy day,'"[91] and later he ponders, "'The doom of choice.'"[92] Like Paul in the *Dune* novels, the characters in *The Lord of the Rings* often seem aware that they are part of the happenings that will become myth. (As Aragorn says to Éomer, "'those who come after will make the legends of our time.'"[93]) Both authors indicate there is something both willed by the characters *and* destined by a greater power than themselves. Aragorn sees this, too—he believes he is part of "fate" and "doom," but he also looks to how his individual decisions will shape this fate. In essence, Tolkien shows readers that whatever role his characters are to play, they must take action. They cannot be idle or passive in their lives, and thus they must be roused to action, like the Shire later. It is not enough to desire good; they (we) need to take an active role in creating good.

The varying communities that Tolkien and Herbert describe and the relationships these communities forge with their environments promote self-reflection. These passages encourage readers to feel and react, which is what mythopoeic fantasy and ecofiction do. Ecoconscious audiences cannot just be passive observers of an objective nature. They are the subjects, the evildoers, and the potential heroes. We feel for the Hobbits and the Atreides, and we also see how easy it is to cross the line between the stewardship of the Ents and the Fremen—that of loving, nurturing, and encouraging growth and independence in all kinds of creatures and natural spaces—and the pride and control of Saruman or the Baron. When we return to our daily existence out of the mythopoeic story, can we use these feelings for a more productive environmental future, one that follows the authors' appreciation of the beauty and value of many different ecosystems and relationships with nature? Like Sam, can we hold onto hope, carrying on even in small ways, even if we think our actions are not as grand or effective as they could be? These are profound questions put forth in Tolkien's and Herbert's writings. Whatever theme or archetype speaks to each of us in these mythopoeic fantasies, the authors' messages of hope, persistence, and goodness come through clearly, sustaining and amplifying these other aspects of their literature.

CHAPTER 4

NATURE'S VOICE

Language in the Legendarium and Duniverse

A significant way in which Tolkien and Herbert engage in mythopoeia is through their invention of new languages and their use of existing ones. Many people have studied their invented languages (the Elvish Linguistic Fellowship, or ELF, is devoted to studying Tolkien's invented languages), and these linguistic flourishes certainly add to the believability of Middle-earth and the Dune planets. However, languages also reinforce the environmental themes identified so far in this study. How Tolkien and Herbert use language reveals the attitudes that they have toward nature and can enrich readers' understanding of these attitudes. In particular, Tolkien's and Herbert's linguistic choices emphasize a sense of enchantment, recovery, and resacralization of nature. Marek Oziewicz notes the unique way in which mythopoeic fantasists employ language: "In its use of and respect for language mythopoeic fantasy aims at what I can best encompass by the term harmony."[1] Tolkien's use of language reveals an environmental theme, especially the names he has created for races, locations, and individual characters. Herbert, however, uses the rhythms of nature in structuring his narratives and engages readers in an ecological "dialogue," as will be explained later. Though the specific ways in which the authors utilize language varies, their common ground is in harmonizing story, language, and environment; such harmony perhaps "reflects mythopoeic authors' holistic conviction about some kind of *harmonia mundi*, a basic unity of life."[2] As this "unity has long been disrupted" in the real world, we can look to "the realm of the mythic imagination" to find it: "From this perspective mythopoeic fantasy may be called a literary search for a harmonious relationship between human beings, between humans and nature and between humans and the Absolute. This search is done in and through words, and words in mythopoeic fantasy are important. . . . [L]inguistic consistency and the power of language to reflect holistically conceived reality are crucial."[3] The Legendarium and the Duniverse offer many models of harmonious and disharmonious relationships between human beings, nature, and "the Absolute"; in previous chapters, I examined many of the word choices the authors draw upon to describe landscapes and human relationships with nature, and below I look more specifically at the meaning behind some of these words.

Tolkien's invented languages are an important part of how he builds Middle-earth; in fact, Tolkien famously claimed to have created his Legendarium around and after the languages, with the places and characters serving the words and not the other way around. Each invented word and name must hold an important place in Tolkien's estimation and a significant semantic purpose. Farah Mendlesohn explores the role language plays in the portal-quest fantasy, focusing particularly on Tolkien's and C. S. Lewis's use of "histories" and the reliability of storytelling. She identifies the necessity of an immersive linguistic experience to convince readers of that Secondary World, that "as readers, we are positioned to be dependent upon what we are told, but both Tolkien and Lewis recognize that if the internal narrative is to convince, it must be sealed from within, not without."[4] Thus, language is an invaluable component in creating mythopoeia. Moreover, the way Tolkien uses language "is directed to the telling. . . . Stories, not just language, are in and of themselves convincing."[5] Finally, Mendlesohn examines how the landscape itself takes part in the linguistic relationship between text and reader, at times "speaking," at other times silent, but always important: "We as readers are also under increasing pressure to pay attention to the moral significance of landscape, that semiosis that encodes the feelings of actors and readers. . . . For . . . Tolkien, landscape was validated as an adventure and character in and of itself."[6] Mendlesohn's claims support this and other chapters' contention, that language and nature are inextricably connected and significant as worldbuilding tools and as powerful in themselves. The following examples highlight some of the words Tolkien selected in world-building that have multiple linguistic antecedents and connotations, which, when examined closely, reveal an environmental meaning that enriches readers' understanding of that particular name and the person/place to which it refers.

Of course, Hobbits are an iconic people within Middle-earth. According to Tom Shippey, the word *Hobbit* comes from *holdbytla,* an Old English construct meaning *hole-builder*.[7] The word *hole* is derived from the Old English word *hollow,* which in turn derives from the Old German word *hohl,* which is pronounced the same as the modern English word *hole.* In Tolkien's imagined Hobbit language, Hobbits refer to themselves as *kudok,* a worn-down version of the word *kud-dukan,* meaning "hole-builder," which is a Gothic construct that Tolkien derived from the prehistoric German word *khulaz*.[8] Incidentally, *khulaz* means "hollow" in prehistoric German. There is an almost circular connection between the word *Hobbit* and these words: *Hobbit* comes from *hole-builder,* and *hole* comes from *hollow,* which comes from *hohl,* which is pronounced *hole,* which is where Hobbits live; evidently, the word *Hobbit* describes the people it represents on multiple levels.[9] More importantly, Tolkien has created a name for these people that connects them to their land and habitations. Their name does not convey their small stature, or their hairy feet, or any of their other idiosyncrasies; instead, their name grounds them clearly as people with a close relationship to their *place.* Indeed, as Flieger observes, "these unshod little people are closer to the earth than their taller relatives, more physically in touch with it and more completely in tune with it,"[10] their bare feet contributing to their identity as farmers and gardeners, "connected to the Earth in so basic a fashion."[11] As readers can see, Tolkien uses language and naming to reinforce the importance of environmental relationships as much as to provide new and delightful linguistic inventions.

Another name carrying an environmental connotation, albeit not necessarily a positive one, is Smeagol, Gollum's original name. Smeagol means *burrowing* or *worming in.*[12] The name comes from the Old English word *smeah,* meaning *penetrating* or *creeping*[13] or *Smygel* (or *Smeagol*), which means *worming in,* which then became *Smial* (pronounced *smile*) in modern English, which means *to burrow.*[14] This is clearly descriptive of Gollum's practice of burrowing deep into the mountains, in the dark, waiting to prey upon such creatures as Hobbits. Readers cannot avoid the animalistic connotations of Gollum, as well, whose lifestyle is similar to that of a mole or a worm, hidden in darkness and stunted by his long habitation in the mountain. Indeed, his very ability to communicate, even his humanity, are affected by his solitude and the corrupting influence of the Ring. As Flieger notes, "Gollum/Smeeagol exemplify Tolkien's use of idiom, dialect, and idiosyncratic speech for purposes of characterization,"[15] reinforcing this chapter's claim that the authors' language directly reinforces their larger purposes in their mythopoeic texts. Gollum's complicated relationship with nature[16] and correspondingly divided humanity even take effect on his speech patterns: "Gollum's childish whinings and mutterings mark him as regressive and infantile; his habitual use of the plural to refer to himself signals his divided character; his rare use of 'I' heralds the infrequent return of his hobbit humanity."[17] As the last chapter explored, environmental relationships are paired with moral ones, and it would seem that linguistic relationships are as well. The language used to describe these characters and that they use to describe themselves expose their personalities and moral qualities in interesting ways.

Gandalf is another significant name in the Legendarium, again reinforcing Tolkien's environmental concerns in naming his characters and places. In this case, the naming of Gandalf associates him with the spiritual realm as well. According to biographer Daniel Grotta, Tolkien revealed the identity of Gandalf, admitting privately to "critic Edmond Fuller in 1962 that 'Gandalf is an angel.'"[18] According to Shippey, Gandalf originates from a name in the Icelandic *Dvevrgatal,* Gandalfr,[19] and David Day adds that "The Old Norse element of Gandalfr, when translated, is Gand—meaning a magical power or the power of Gand—that is, 'astral travelling.'"[20] Gandalf, then, takes on the meaning of a celestial body, a star traveling the heavens. In addition, while Gandalf has many origins (including Merlin of the Celts, Odin of the Norsemen, Woden of the Early Germans, Mercury of the Romans, Hermes of the Greeks, and Thoth of the Egyptians), "all are linked with magic, sorcery, arcane knowledge, and secret doctrine."[21] If interpreting Gandalf as an angelic being, readers can see the "manifestation" or revealing of Gandalf as an angel when he transforms from Gandalf the Gray to Gandalf the White. Gandalf's Elven name is *Mithrandir,* meaning Gray Wanderer, but Gandalf in Old Norse means, as Noel translates it, "sorcerer elf,"[22] a clear sign of his "goodness."[23] Gandalf's transformation into the White Wizard also calls to mind his earlier incarnation as a Maia, a less powerful "holy one" from the cosmological beginnings of Middle-earth (which was then called Arda and created by Eru Ilúvatar, the All-Powerful divinity[24]). This identity is pivotal to his environmental relationship because, "although Gandalf aligns his own mission in Middle-earth with Ilúvatar's purpose for creation, he never forgets that it is Ilúvatar's creation, Ilúvatar's purpose, and Ilúvatar's power from which his own is derived."[25] For Jeffers, Gandalf's awareness of his power and purpose allows him to maintain the necessary ecological humility to be an effective servant-steward on Middle-earth,[26] unlike his Maia counterpart, Saruman.

The linguistic inspiration for Saruman quite obviously reflects the negative environmental relationship this character has, and perhaps a clever reader could predict the betrayal awaiting Gandalf at the hands of his former friend. The name Saruman is taken from the Old English root *searu-*, meaning *treachery* or *cunning* and similar to his Maia name, Curumo, meaning *skillful one*.[27] Noel glosses the name similarly, claiming it translates as "crafty man" from the Old English for "craft," "device," or "wile."[28] These descriptions connect with his love of machinery and industry—the wheels and gears riddling the land around Isengard and the slave pits where his weaponry is crafted—and they also fit his past as servant to Aulë the Smith, one of the great Valar (or angelic beings of a higher order than the Maiar). The Rohirrim name Isengard fits the descriptions of its land, deriving from an Old English word, *geard,* meaning "iron yard" or "enclosure."[29] In addition, Saruman's name is "an Old English construct meaning Man of Pain"[30] and also comes from an Old Norse or Icelandic root, meaning *filth, dung,* or *uncleanness.* While this root suggests a connection to the earth, it is one paradoxically characterized by *disconnection,* a kind of mythic dissociation like that discussed in chapter 1, which sees nature as other and therefore allows Saruman to feel justified in dominating it.[31]

Thus, characters like Sauron and Saruman are tied to the land in a twisted, torturous relationship that yields none of the fruits of life, growth, and renewal that come with a healthful environmental relationship. So while Sauron and Saruman "may hate the land . . . they need that connection to it to gain their ideal self-actualization" (via domination); however, as they "dominate more and more oppressively, the connection between themselves and their places is strained."[32] Flieger, too, sees how Saruman's ethical decisions strain him: "In his overweening pride, Saruman has broken himself, not, like Frodo, by yielding to a cause greater than himself but by trying to impose himself upon the cause, by endeavoring to control rather than submit."[33] As Gollum represents a divided self, torn between his Hobbit humanity and his "burrowing" animalism, Saruman fragments himself while imagining he has achieved greatness. Saruman's fate is no better than Gollum's either: "Saruman, in the inflation of his precious self, knows a little, but thinks he knows more, and that is enough. The very opposite is the case. He does not know, and does not realize he does not know. A world of psychological, moral, and spiritual differences separates him from Frodo."[34] Interestingly, as Flieger has analyzed, both Gollum and Saruman serve as distorted reflections of Frodo; Gollum is of course a constant reminder of Frodo's potential to become like him, feeble and overcome by the Ring, while Saruman is like an "inflated" opposite of Frodo in pride and vanity where Frodo embodies humility and modesty. Overall, the various origins and meanings of Saruman's name paint a grim portrait of all aspects of his existence, including environmental and moral, and this portrait suggests that his treacherous cunning will lead to others' and his own pain, lowering him from exalted angelic being to something worse than dirt.

The philological origins of Sauron's name have an equally foreboding quality as Saruman's. The name Sauron means *abominable* or *The Abhorred* in High Elvish,[35] and is "also suggestive of *sauros*," meaning *lizard* in Greek.[36] It is not much of a stretch to see the connection between lizards, snakes, and dragons (all traditionally villainous literary/mythological creatures, even with overtones of Satan). And Morgoth, Sauron's former name, means *The Black Enemy*. These connotations of darkness, antagonism, and abhorrence combine to fit how Sauron interacts with his environment. He, Saruman, and the Orcs all use the land to take "power over" through exploitation and enslavement. As Jeffers reminds readers, that Sauron is "positioned as morally bankrupt within *The Lord of the Rings* suggests that this approach to one's environment is similarly void of integrity."[37] Moreover, "Marjorie Burns argues eloquently that 'the greatest evil in Tolkien's view is "possessiveness," a sin which includes simple materialism as well as domination, enslavement, and arbitrary control; and these, of course, are qualities which may be as manifest in those who inherit power as in those who acquire it by force, stealth, or deception.'"[38] Sauron is trapped in his concern over "Self" and unable to make any legitimate connections with his land or with other beings; in fact, as Jeffers has noted, Sauron is so absorbed with his Self that he has literally separated that Self from a material manifestation, existing almost immaterially so as to remove the physical interactions and interconnectivity required of other living beings in Middle-earth. In this sense, the "Black Enemy" also suggests the darkness or void that the absence of his body has created. Flieger discusses Sauron's status as "external darkness,"[39] the opposite or complementary force to the Elves of Light and other forms of "splintered light" that emerge in *The Silmarillion*.[40]

Place names also indicate Tolkien's environmental vision. Mordor is derived from Middle English *murther,* which comes from Old English *morthor,* which is akin to Old High German *mord,* and all of which mean *murder*.[41] In Tolkien's Sindarin language, the place means "Dark Country,"[42] from two words meaning *dark* and *land*. Perhaps of all the words explored so far, this one has the bleakest and most violent meaning; truly, Mordor is a land of death and murder, and it seems a fitting way to describe the kind of environmental model set forth in Sauron's domain: "Mordor is the cancer of Middle-earth. It continues to exist, but there is no known cure for it, and it spreads out from its original place. Just as Sauron is consumption, his land is consumptive. There is no cure for either. Both are already dead."[43] Interestingly, the land was already "dead" before Sauron set up his habitation there,[44] and like Sauron's attitude toward nature, it appealed to him because of its many "natural fortifications," keeping the land and its inhabitants separated from others.

Moria, too, has an interesting linguistic interpretation. Flieger looks at the name in different languages, including the Dwarvish name, Khazad-Dûm; the Old English name, Dwarrowdelf; the Sindarin (Elvish) name, Moria; and the Common Speech name, Black Pit.[45] According to Flieger, each name has its own unique connotation and effect on the listener/reader. The Dwarvish name means Mansions of the Khazad, meaning "the Dwarves. It is their name for their own place as seen through their own eyes; it reflects their sense of their own grandeur."[46] The Old English name, however, means Dwarf-delving, changing the grandness of *mansions* into *digging* or *excavation,* while the Common Speech describes their home as even less important: "a black pit is for falling into, either through accident or despair."[47] Finally, the Sindarin name is not much better—it derives from two roots meaning *dark* and *void* or *abyss,* "suggesting dark, bottomless emptiness or even a black hole."[48] These final meanings in particular connote an overwhelming consumption—being swallowed up by the dark void. Jeffers identifies the Dwarves' "power from" relationship to the land as a form of consumption/consumerism. While the Dwarves do not represent the kind of irrevocably destructive environmental interactions of Saruman or Sauron, their connection to their lands is problematic: "Dwarves aren't concerned with 'having enough'; they must have enough and to spare, many times over. It is not without reasons that Elves often accuse Dwarves of greed. . . . [T]he resources under the Mountain are not appreciated for themselves, but are instead used to signify the wealth of Dwarves. They gain status from their resources."[49] Dwarves have the inherent capacity to love and appreciate their surroundings (Jeffers notes Gimli's unique love for Galadriel as an important destabilization of the "power from" model), but as a race, they need to embrace consumerism instead. This pattern perhaps rings familiar to readers as a human tendency, too. We often acquire resources as signifiers, as markers of status, or to satiate our own desire for "enough and to spare": the "abyss" of Moria calls to us, too. Like the environment these names describe, each moniker carries a unique interpretation, and "such differences work on the reader to convey a world richly complex with meanings, all the more arresting because these meanings rub against one another, sometimes overlap or compete."[50] Flieger identifies this "fluidity" as a way in which readers "create" Middle-earth alongside Tolkien, another distinct way in which mythopoeic fantasy empowers its readers with a sub-creative capacity. Moria stands as another example of how closely intertwined language and descriptions of nature are, and all the examples provided reinforce how carefully Tolkien fit his invented words to their places and peoples, matching names and qualities in such a way as to reveal, among other things, the environmental attitudes inherent in them.

Fortunately, though, names can also take on positive meanings that fit healthier environmental relationships. Frodo's name, for example, connects directly with the fate of the Shire, both culturally and ecologically. Frodo comes from the Old English *fród*, meaning *wise, prudent*, or *sage*[51] and *freoda, protector, defender*, and *freodo, peace* and *security*.[52] These meanings combine to suggest an interconnection between wisdom, protection, and peace: "In Old English and Scandinavian mythology, the name Frodo (or Froda, Frothi, Frotha) is most often connected with a peacemaker. In the Old English epic *Beowulf* there is Froda the powerful King of the Heathobards who attempts to make peace between the Danes and Bards. In Norse mythology there is a King Frothi who rules a realm of peace and prosperity. Also, in Icelandic texts we find the expression *Frotha-frith*, meaning 'Frothi's Peace' with reference to a legendary 'Age of Peace and Wealth.'"[53] From this information, Day draws a connection to Frodo as peacemaker, an identity he takes on following the War of the Ring. After the Hobbits' return to and scouring of the Shire, the following year is the "Year of Great Plenty," "when the harvest was more bountiful than any in history"[54] and which ushered in an "Age of Peace and Wealth," again ensuring the Shire's environmental thriving. Here, Tolkien suggests that peaceful interactions with other beings and the land yield fruitful results. Moreover, Frodo as peacemaker represents a profound and complex relationship with the land, a kind of prefiguration of Christ in his sacrificial humility:[55] "Frodo sacrifices not only his feather bed back home in Bag End, but also any hope for peace or rest for himself anywhere in Middle-earth."[56] From Frodo's example, readers can derive an environmental and moral message:

It is this same attitude of humility and self-abnegation that again appears in characters with a positive connection with the environment. Close readers may begin to see that, in *The Lord of the Rings,* the way one treats one's environment is reflective of a characteristic greater than mere land-use politics. For the characters in Tolkien's *legendarium,* it is indicative of the way one lives one's life, and why. Ecological humility is just one part of the great virtue of charity, which virtue covers a multitude of (ecological) sins and transgressions.[57]

As Dickerson and Evans recognize, in some ways, Sam bears the larger burden of staying in Middle-earth and putting the hard work into reclaiming the Shire's bounty, offering a remarkable example of stewardship that readers can look to as an environmental model.[58] However, Jeffers makes an equally relevant point in the above passage—that "humility and self-abnegation" have their place in Middle-earth (and the primary world) as attitudes engendering a "positive connection with the environment." I would add that these different examples of environmental care as parts of the "great virtue of charity" support what the previous chapters have advocated—that within the Legendarium and the Duniverse there is room for many kinds of valuable environments and ways to relate to those environments. Frodo's is yet another example added to these rich stories.

Like Tolkien, Herbert provides many different examples of nature and how to connect to it, and language (in its many forms, verbal and nonverbal) was also a pivotal force in his world-building. His creative process frequently revolved around nature: his son notes that Herbert would frequently begin building scenes and dialogue in the *Dune* chronicles using poetry, especially haikus, which often have nature as their topic.[59] Like an ecocritic, he often used observational writing to draw inspiration, which, combined with his interest in Zen Buddhism, helped him investigate "nonverbal interaction—understanding and saying things without words."[60] Linguistic decisions large and small emerged in composing his Duniverse, as even the words used to name the planets took on careful choosing and significance: "The planet commonly known as Dune is called Arrakis by the ruling nobles, a harsh-sounding name that is suggestive of an inhospitable place. And inhospitable it is, under the short-sighted, usurping control of the noblemen. The very name 'Dune' is like a great sigh, suggestive of a faraway, exotic land. [Fremen] . . . use an unauthorized planet name in defiance of authority."[61] Clearly, like Tolkien, Herbert engaged seriously with language, and readers should not overlook the significance of how language reinforces the themes of his mythopoeic writings; Herbert also created his own languages and names, utilizing them as support for intensive and ecocritical world-building: "The use of proper names is also a 'particularly efficient way to create a sense of place without resorting to lengthy descriptions'. . . . Therefore, names are a type of shortcut to 'capture the feel of a place' or a certain time period 'without losing the reader in a descriptive thicket' . . . Herbert quickly lays the foundation for the setting of *Dune* through names and so facilitates the world-building process."[62] This chapter will therefore focus both on some of these invented names and their ecocritical significance, and holistically on Herbert's linguistic choices, particularly in how he structures *Dune* and utilizes dialogue to focus the reader's attention on the environment.

Kara Kennedy observes how Herbert's choice of names takes inspiration from identifiable sources, striking a balance between "difference" and "familiarity" that will convince readers of the imaginative otherness of an invented story while not estranging readers too greatly (in her study, Kennedy engages with Adam Roberts's review of science fiction definitions and the need for cognitive estrangement).[63] Kennedy writes, "To avoid this kind of alienation and yet still develop a world different from reality, Herbert deliberately chooses names that already exist or are slightly altered and so evoke recognizable time periods, environments, religions, and cultures, and construct the illusion of a universe that exists beyond the borders of the story itself."[64] I see the effect of these choices as mirroring that of Tolkien's, in that his inspiration from actual ancient and medieval languages, and his subsequent invented languages, "evoke [the] recognizable" yet also imbue the Legendarium with "the illusion of a universe that exists beyond the borders of the story itself." The protagonists' names in Herbert's Duniverse similarly make clear their ethical and environmental attitudes. Paul, "derived from the Latin *Paulus*, meaning 'small,' . . . carries a link with Saint Paul, the first-century Roman Jew who helped found the Christian Church through his missionary work."[65] Paul's name suggests the transformative, indeed "religious" work that he will accomplish on Arrakis, politically, environmentally, and culturally.

Paul's mother's name, Jessica, "means 'one who looks forth' and is also Biblical."[66] The connotation of "vision" and "sight" associated with her name corresponds to her role as powerful Bene Gesserit (and eventual Reverend Mother) gifted with skills beyond the common person, as indeed does the name Bene Gesserit itself (evoking "good" and "Jesuit").[67] This chapter will later detail the ways in which Jessica evolves an ecocritical consciousness, though not quite to the degree that Paul does. And their surname, Atreides, "recalls the mythic Greek figure of Atreus, 'father of Agamemnon and Menelaus'. . . . Such legendary figures 'abound in subcreated mythologies, their deeds shaping their worlds and their histories.'"[68] While Atreides has mythopoeic resonance, it is significant that Paul adopts the name of Muad'Dib among the Fremen, rather than Atreides, which Kennedy claims "signals his transition into a position of strength and leadership. It is the name of the resourceful desert mouse on Dune, foreshadowing Paul's ability to adapt to his environment as well as providing an additional tie-in to the aforementioned Latin meaning of his name, 'small.'"[69] This choice ties Paul to the land and its creatures, as well as to his new Fremen community.[70] (In contrast, Kennedy observes the overtones of Cold War–era Russia in Vladimir Harkonnen's name, an obvious shorthand of "otherness" and values at odds with the Greco-Roman Atreides family.) While not a complete list of names in the Duniverse and their significance, these examples begin to help us see how Herbert utilizes names in his mythopoeic world-building and as indicators of ecocritical consciousness in a manner akin to Tolkien.

Scholar Donald Palumbo observes that Herbert also uses language in an ecocritically conscious manner via structure: Herbert structured his narrative according to rhythms of nature, at times increasing the intensity in the pacing of events or dialogue, at other points moving slowly through descriptions and characters' thoughts. Palumbo identifies how Herbert purposefully structured his novels to echo chaos theory, for example, explicitly and implicitly reinforcing the series' ecological theme.[71] Others have recognized Herbert's writing as "ecological semantics," which "involves the relation and interaction of the users or communicators of language in a manner similar to how environmental ecology involves the relation and interaction of organisms and their environment."[72] Therefore, like Tolkien, Herbert makes deliberate linguistic choices in his mythopoeic fantasy that emphasize nature's significance. Herbert was especially interested in the connections between language, power, and the environment, and we can examine some of these connections in the first novel, *Dune*.[73] Biographer and critic William F. Touponce offers a perspective on how significant ecology is in Herbert's writing: "Ecology was no longer simply a theme, but had become an aesthetic strategy, the author being one voice among many others in an evolving system of ideas. . . . The primary theme of *Dune* is, then ecology. . . . To read *Dune* critically is to read it in ecological terms, as the text becomes the element of the environment to which the individual responds and vice versa."[74] Touponce confirms the inextricable link between ecology and the novel: one cannot read the text without engaging in the ecological on some level. Therefore, through a sustained close reading of the text, readers can better understand the "aesthetic strategy" Herbert uses and see how the author's use of ecology is essential to the *Dune* chronicles as unique mythopoeic works—as in Tolkien's legendarium, language becomes inextricably linked with environmental relationships, and ecology provides a unifying thread through which to understand the novels' various themes.

The very language that Herbert uses to craft *Dune* suggests an environmental presence at work within the narrative. Herbert saw an inseparable relationship between ecology and language, one that affirms life and its potentials: "His firmest belief was that the meaning of human life emerges through language, itself a mirror of the ecosystems in which life has evolved."[75] This "firm belief" unites several concepts at work in the Duniverse: the importance of what is human, the ecosystems that act upon and interact with humanity, and the ways in which the environment tests humanity and its potential for progress. It seems necessary that the language employed by the author and the characters should also reflect the environment and its influence on Paul, the character in *Dune* (besides the Fremen) who develops the closest relationship to nature and serves as one of readers' most positive environmental role models.

Like Tolkien, Herbert's avid interest in language and linguistics is clearly present throughout his literary works; moreover, critics have found a musical influence in his writing. O'Reilly dubs *Dune* a "polyphonic novel,"[76] what Abrams explains to be "an instance of a narrative . . . which interweaves main plot and a multiplicity of subplots into an intricately interrelated structure."[77] In his analysis of Edmund Spencer's *The Faerie Queene*, C. S. Lewis recognizes this relationship between plot/subplots as having a musical quality similar to "contemporary Elizabethan music, in which two or more diverse melodies are carried on simultaneously,"[78] and Herbert indeed compares his own work to a fugue (see the next paragraph for a discussion of that fugal quality). Like a musical piece, these various literary components stand simultaneously as unique and individual elements while also contributing to the success of the piece as a complete and harmonious composition. Herbert's use of language provides readers with insight into this polyphony of environment or ecological fugue, yet another rich aspect of the *Dune* chronicles that, like Tolkien's legendarium, set them apart as arguably ecocritical works.

As readers examine *Dune* and the larger structural choices that Herbert makes, it is hard to overlook the novel's rhythmic flow as it rises and falls through character's emotions and actions, plot development, and dialogue. Herbert's conscious choice to build in this rhythmical quality offers interesting interpretations: "[Herbert] is convinced that the sound of a passage is subconsciously reconstructed by the reader even though he reads silently, and furthermore, that it has a powerful unconscious effect."[79] Evidently, Herbert combines his conscious efforts to create a subconscious reception from his readers, and perhaps this effort is related to his enduring belief in narrative as a way of incorporating language, conversation, and music as a collective unit. In the collection of Herbert's own articles titled *The Maker of Dune* (1987), the author explains how he understands his novel to be similar to a musical composition, expanding upon the polyphonic nature of *Dune*:

> Enter the fugue. In music, the fugue is usually based on a single theme that is played many different ways. Sometimes there are free voices that do fanciful dances around the interplay. There can be secondary themes and contrasts in harmony, rhythm, and melody. From the moment a single voice introduces the primary theme, however, the whole is woven into a single fabric. What were my instruments in this fugue? Images, conflicts, things that turn upon themselves and become something quite different, myth figures and strange creatures from the depths of our common heritage, products of our technological evolution, our desires and our fears.[80]

Based on Herbert's assertions, readers can view the novel's other themes as both complementary and contrasting "voices" that "interplay" with the primary theme: the environment. In a sense, then, ecology is the pivotal "glue" holding these novels together. The environment seems to be the single theme that is played in many ways—the primary theme from which the secondary themes find their source, therefore allowing them to act as free voices, fancifully dancing around the central theme and providing a depth and intricacy that comprise the chronicles' narratives.

Therefore, from the core melody of environment, the secondary tune of language interplays in intricate and skillful ways, underscoring how important the core melody is, as well as how important Paul's need for mastery of language is in his rise as an effective and ecoconscious leader. By examining

Herbert's use of language in *Dune,* one can better understand the thought patterns and environmental choices that motivate the various characters, Paul especially. Speculative fiction author Neal Stephenson identifies language's ability to shape cognition: "We've got two kinds of language in our heads. The kind we're using now is acquired. It patterns our brains as we're learning it. But there's also a tongue that's based in the deep structures of the brain that everyone shares. These structures consist of basic neural circuits that have to exist in order to allow our brains to acquire higher languages."[81] Stephenson recognizes that language has an innate nature that humanity shares, which enables higher languages and thought patterns to be learned. Paul discovers a full utilization of this innate language: he comprehends and adapts to the necessary thought patterns and languages of the desert, including dialects of the Fremen and ecological dialects. Through this innate linguistic ability, Paul is able to "pattern" his brain to the structures of Dune's languages and therefore obtain and maintain the necessary power to become leader of Arrakis.[82]

As the Reverend Mother speaks to Paul of how he will need to survive the desert planet, she makes a significant point regarding the power of language in contributing to Paul's success as a leader. More importantly, the Reverend Mother's statement on mastery addresses Paul's future survival: "'Then she said a good ruler has to learn his world's language, that it's different for every world. And I thought she meant that they didn't speak Galach on Arrakis, but she said that wasn't it at all. She said she meant the language of the rocks and growing things, the language you don't hear just with your ears. And I said that's what Dr. Yueh calls the Mystery of Life.'"[83] For Paul, there is language in the very elements of nature that he must be aware of as the Kwisatz Haderach (the Bene Gesserit's prophesied "savior"), and he does indeed grasp this language, in part aided by his prescient visions, in part by his innate gifts as an Atreides. Herbert himself ruminates on this topic, recognizing that "words are a vehicle of power."[84] By calling it "the language you don't hear just with your ears" and "the Mystery of Life," Herbert subtly imbues this form of communication with a mystical property, reinforcing a sense of transcendence that results from a closer relationship with one's environment (similar to what Paul experienced in the desert, or in encountering sandworms, as chapter 2 asserted). For Paul, the words that he understands from Arrakis lend him the *power* of his environment, as he learns to both listen to and speak with the planet.

As the novel progresses, the planet does indeed speak to Paul, and his awareness of this ecological language shows his qualities as a perceptive listener to the "musicality" of Arrakis that Herbert builds into his novel. As the Reverend Mother has explained to Paul, there is a language of the "rocks and growing things,"[85] a language that Paul comes to perceive and appreciate, listening and interpreting closely. The author shows this clearly, even when Paul and his mother are vulnerable and abandoned in the desert following Leto's death:[86] "Paul continued to stare across the basin. He inhaled, sensed the softly cutting contralto smell of sage climbing the night. The predatory bird—he thought of it as the way of the desert. It had brought a stillness to the basin so unuttered that the blue-milk moonlight could almost be heard flowing across sentinel saguaro and spiked paintbrush. There was a low humming of light here more basic in its harmony than any other music in his universe."[87] Herbert effectually conveys a calm moment of reflection for Paul, one that highlights Paul's propensity for minute observation, sensing the speech (albeit primarily nonverbal) of nature: the sights—"Paul continued to stare"; the smells—he "sensed the ... smell of sage"; and the sounds, heard and unheard—"a stillness ... [in which] moonlight could almost be heard"; all pieces in a musical composition of nature ("contralto," "humming," "harmony," "music"). The stillness and gentle musicality of nature contrasts with the violence inherent in an untamed place: the predatory bird that swoops down and takes hold of the mouse,[88] a metaphor for the "way of the desert" as it takes hold of Paul Maud'Dib (again, the Fremen word for mouse). The hero is being absorbed by this planet through its distinctive "language" of ecology.

As Herbert researched desert ecology for his journalism efforts, he began to see complex connections between nearly all aspects of life, claiming that he "could begin to see the shape of a global problem, no part of it separated from any other—social ecology, political ecology, economic ecology. . . . It's an open-ended list which has never closed."[89] This saturation of ecology found its way into Herbert's creative output, and Touponce perceives an important relationship between ecology and communication, with Herbert's environmental concerns functioning as a uniting force with his interest in religion: "He began to see that all of his research both into the ecology of deserts as well as comparative religions provided him with enormously interesting material for a novel if he could put the two discourses—religious and ecological—together in a contrapuntal manner, playing one against the other. What better medium than science fiction, which provides an imaginary space of extrapolation where discourses ordinarily found separate in reality can be made to converse with one another?"[90] Interestingly, Touponce uses the word "discourse" to describe the opportunity that science fiction gives its readers. Language and communication are at the heart of Herbert's purpose in his writings, allowing his audience to achieve an awareness and discussion of the aims of ecology, language, heroics and the dangers of superheroes, and other concerns that Herbert had. Herbert's use of language throughout *Dune* unmistakably points to the pivotal role the environment plays throughout his novel: specific word choices, conversations between characters that operate on multiple levels, and the actual language he has created for his world. Like Tolkien, Herbert pays painstaking attention to detail and authenticity in his languages (both created and preexistent), which in turn contributes to the detail and authenticity of his novels, immersing readers in these mythopoeic fantasies' ecocritical concerns.

Clearly, the environment is a pivotal shaping force in the language of *Dune*, both the language used in a more general sense to narrate the plot and the language discovered by characters as inherent to the planet itself. Linguist Guy Deutscher identifies the relationship between language and one's physical location in *Through the Language Glass* (2010). According to Deutscher, the geographic location of a person or people greatly determines how thought and linguistic patterns develop. He explains that nature indirectly affects how one thinks and speaks, combined as well with how one was raised, "through the mediation of culture."[91] Deutscher asserts there is "a compelling case that the relation between language and spatial thinking is not just correlation but causation, and that one's mother tongue affects how one thinks about space."[92] It is clear that Paul is affected by the "mediation of culture" to which he has been exposed, and that this combination of heredity and environment equips Paul with the necessary linguistic structure through which to operate successfully as an ecoconscious leader, and part of this linguistic structure that Deutscher identifies is exemplified in what Herbert dubs the "Voice."

The Bene Gesserit organization trains their own in how to control others with particular semantic and vocal choices, and Paul employs the Voice to even greater success than other characters, including the Reverend Mother Gaius Helen and Lady Jessica.[93] By using the Voice, Paul and the Bene Gesserit (and, later, the Fremen) are able to control people and situations through secondary meanings and implied directives. Herbert's invention of the Bene Gesserit "Voice" also has links to a fantasy and mythopoeic fantasy tradition:

"The idea of a right sound at a right time under the right conditions producing a desired effect lies as much at the roots of magical thinking as it does at the roots of religion, traditional literature, and mythopoeic fantasy."[94] In Tolkien's writings as much as Herbert's, a "right sound at a right time" frequently occurs during important scenes, such as in opening the door to Moria, or Gandalf's magical phrases uttered at just the opportune moment.[95]

Brian Herbert chronicles his father's interest in language and its subliminal power in *Dreamer of Dune*: "Dad learned much of this in studies of semantics he made for the purpose of writing political speeches. Politicians had to be especially careful about word selection in order to avoid alienating large blocks of voters. And in order to appeal to them."[96] Paul has been raised from birth with the dual agendas of the ducal line and the Bene Gesserit order, both of which are forces political in nature. It is only logical that Paul would be consistently mindful of his speech, choosing his words to fit each location and audience. However, as Paul develops as a leader, so do his skills with language and Voice. While the Atreides host a "dinner party" (an important scene that this chapter uses as a sustained example) for important guests of Arrakis, Paul uses some of his limited skills with Voice training; though limited, they are still powerful: he understands when and how to utilize just the right anecdotes and intonations of voice to elicit reactions from others. When dealing with a banker in particular, Paul demonstrates this power and authority, causing Jessica to recognize the "brittle riposte quality of her training exposed in his voice"[97] as he stands up to the boasts the banker throws out. Paul reveals his innate understanding of politically delicate situations, and he acts upon this understanding: "Paul had marked the falseness in his dinner companion's voice, saw that his mother was following the conversation with Bene Gesserit intensity. On impulse, he decided to play the foil, draw the exchange out."[98] Here and above, Herbert uses fencing/weaponized language to describe Paul's ability with Voice, its "riposte quality" disarming his enemies and showing his formidable skills. Paul engages those in authority without fear or hesitation but instead with a perspicuity and precision that belie his age. Nevertheless, at this point in the novel, Paul has not yet mastered the Voice, a fact drawn to light when Paul and his mother are taken captive by the Harkonnens.[99] Paul is still on the brink of realizing his identity as Kwisatz Haderach, and it is his environmental surroundings that bring out his latent ecolinguistic qualities.

As Paul grows in his prescient visions, he likewise grows in his ability to utilize language to its full potential. As he and Jessica wait in a stilltent (a moisture-preserving emergency structure) and mourn the Duke's death, Paul undergoes a transformative experience that illuminates his "terrible purpose" and prescient visions. As he speaks to his mother, the change in his voice/Voice is evident: "*There's no more childhood in his voice,* she thought.... 'Listen to me,' he said.... The terrifying *presence* of his voice brooked no dispute."[100] After this episode, Paul no longer struggles with his power over Voice or language. He has passed this hurdle in his journey as leader. In subsequent chapters, several examples follow that demonstrate his linguistic power, whether in seemingly trivial conflicts or in life-altering challenges. For instance, when Paul must deal with Jamis's widow (after defeating Jamis in single combat), he employs his power of speech to successful effect: "Paul had registered enough of her to have a first approximation. He felt the impatience of the troop, knew many things were being delayed here.... He faced Harah, pitched his voice with tone and tremolo to accent her fear and awe.... She backed away two steps, casting a frightened glance at Stilgar. 'He has the weirding voice,' she husked."[101] Herbert reinforces the Fremens' superstitious nature through Paul's use of voice control and semantics, ennobling Paul to the tribe as a mystical leader. Later, when Paul must "change the way" of the Fremen to stop the duels between tribe members, he has a crucial test of his power over language: "Paul hurled his voice at them in anger. ... Paul spoke dryly, probing the emotional undercurrents.... Jessica heard the subtle intonations as he used the powers of Voice she had taught him."[102] Here again, Jessica—sensitive to the use of Voice—understands the control Paul has. Soon after this incident, Paul's linguistic control reaches an emotional climax as he must convince his dear friend and teacher Gurney that his mother did not betray the late Duke (as Gurney mistakenly believes); at this point Paul demonstrates his full powers of Voice: "'Be quiet,' Paul said, and the monotone stillness of his words carried more command than Jessica had ever heard in another voice. *He has the Great Control,* she thought.... Hearing her son, Jessica marveled at the awareness in him, the penetrating insight of his intelligence."[103] Paul understands how to utilize the Voice, both to larger audiences (as in his crucial persuasion of the Fremen to give up the regressive practice of ritual duels, which weaken their tribes) and in personal situations, as he convinces Gurney not to murder his mother and instead hear the truth of what he says.

This sensitivity to truth finds frequent repetition throughout *Dune* as Herbert positions Paul as a vehicle for truth (in his personal life, Herbert was known to have a strong desire for and commitment to honesty in all circumstances). Truth and falsity function as thematic elements throughout the novel alongside light and darkness (both literal and figurative), and these themes often coincide with or are underscored by the characters' physical environments. For example, the Baron and the Emperor are surrounded by intrigue and false information, used to deceive each other and maintain personal power. Clandestine meetings and treacherous plans frequently take place outside of Arrakis, or at least outside of the open desert, in dimly lit, hidden rooms. However, the Fremen and Paul—always surrounded by and mindful of nature, as most of their scenes take place in the desert, quite literally a completely open place—strive for truth, openness, and understanding, even when using subtleties of language. Much of this emphasis on true meaning can be traced to Herbert's studies of linguistic patterns and underlying messages, as identified by his son: "Semantics of the time recognized the existence of 'metamessages' beneath the actual spoken words—messages that would not be picked up if the words were merely displayed on paper. Something in the tone of voice revealed what was really meant. Perhaps the person didn't actually mean what was being said, or of two meanings, the normally secondary meaning was really primary. This was linked to my father's studies of the subconscious and to his analysis of subliminal advertising."[104] From the beginning of the novel, the Reverend Mother knows that Paul senses truth in language—he sees through "metamessages" to comprehend root motivations, the speaker's true meaning. This skill reveals another dimension to his status as an ecoconscious leader. It is only through his time spent on Arrakis—the environment influencing him—that he reaches these heights of skill, particularly in the novel's last chapter. In *Dune*'s framed structure, Paul faces the Reverend Mother again, but this time, he reveals his true power, an identity that was only guessed at in the beginning of the novel:

> "Try your tricks on me, old witch," Paul said. "Where's your gom jabbar? Try looking into that place where you dare not look! You'll find me there staring out at you!" . . . "Jessica!" the old woman screamed. "Silence him!" . . . "Silence!" Paul roared. The word seemed to take substance as it twisted through the air between them under Paul's control. . . . "I remember your gom jabbar," Paul said. "You remember mine. I can kill you with a word." The Fremen around the hall glanced knowingly at each other. Did the legend not say: "*And his word shall carry death eternal to those who stand against righteousness.*"[105]

For Paul, language has become more than just a formless entity: it is tangible, a physical force of power and control—control over people, places, and situations. Environment and language, both shaping the other, are now pivotal ingredients of Paul's identity and essential elements of his qualifications as an ethical, eco-conscious leader.[106]

The environment itself is of course pivotal in Paul's role as eloquent politician and leader: the spice permeating Arrakis is a catalyst for his web of prescient visions, which in turn enable him to know which words and traditional sayings to employ when faced with precarious challenges to his leadership skills. When Liet-Kynes, the unofficial leader of the Fremen, assesses him, Paul almost unconsciously knows which words to use to cement his status as the Fremens' foretold "messiah":

> On impulse, Paul called to mind a quotation from the O. C. Bible, said: "The gift is the blessing of the giver." The words rang out overloud in the still air. The Fremen escort . . . leaped up from their squatting repose. . . . One cried out "Lisan al-Gaib!" . . . Kynes passed a hard glare over the Duke and Paul, said: "Most of the desert natives here are a superstitious lot. Pay no attention to them. They mean no harm." But he thought of the words of the legend: *"They will greet you with Holy Words and your gifts will be a blessing."*[107]

This passage supports the intersection of nature and the numinous identified in previous chapters; here and elsewhere, Paul utilizes religious language as a way of securing trust and proving himself as a worthy environmental advocate. Paul's earlier encounter with Kynes was also significant in allowing the planetologist to assess Paul's potential as the Fremen's chosen leader, which—most importantly—includes Paul's ability to lead the Fremen to an ecological paradise. By choosing his words carefully, Paul impresses Kynes and the Fremen people, especially by suggesting his near-mythic status. When Paul duels Jamis and must take Jamis's water (the actual water from his body, drained during a ceremonial funeral rite), he again demonstrates his ecolinguistic sensitivity: "Presently Paul recalled the words of 467 Kalima in Yueh's O. C. Bible. He said: 'From water does all life begin.' Jessica stared at him. *Where did he learn that quotation?* she asked herself. *He hasn't studied the mysteries.*"[108] Paul's innate knowledge lends itself to each situation with which he is presented, and this time his words combine his "wisdom" as hero (using mystical texts to support his identity within Fremen myth) with carefully chosen nature imagery (the timeless connection between water and life). Jessica understands that Paul has struck upon something special, that he has not formally learned the "mysteries" of the Orange Catholic Bible, or life, or whichever mysteries she is contemplating in this scene—yet Paul knows them nonetheless. His status as a protagonist sensitive to concerns of religion, ecology, and language is consistently reaffirmed by Herbert.

Another example of the power of language in *Dune* can be found in the trial that the sandstorm presents Paul and Jessica in the middle of the novel. This episode provides essential fodder for Herbert to present Paul from a multifaceted viewpoint: it tests his abilities by challenging his mental strength; it demonstrates how Paul understands and respects the shaping force of nature, both within his own circumstances and in a larger, metaphorical sense; and now it offers several key passages about Paul's relationship with language. After Paul successfully navigates the storm, he reflects on how the Bene Gesserit litany against fear aided him:

> Paul sensed himself trembling on the verge of a revelation. He shivered. The sensation was magnetic and terrifying, and he found himself caught on the question of what caused this trembling awareness. Part of it, he felt, was the spice-saturated diet of Arrakis. But he thought part of it could be the litany, as though the words had a power of their own. "*I shall not fear . . .*" Cause and effect: He was alive despite malignant forces, and he felt himself poised on a brink of self-awareness that could not have been without the litany's magic. Words from the Orange Catholic Bible rang through his memory: "*What senses do we lack that we cannot see or hear another world all around us?*"[109]

Paul sees the power that words have—a kind of control outside of the physical world, yet they influence his internal being. And one should note the imagery that Herbert employs: Paul is "poised on the brink," on the verge or precipice of "revelation" and "self-awareness." This language necessitates that the reader envision Paul on the top of a cliff, and that as he becomes more aware and experienced, he is plunged into these symbolic revelations. It sounds as though Paul is choosing to take this plunge, but when someone falls off a cliff, he or she must surrender control. Paul encounters this freely given choice with a lack of control, a vulnerability to the forces around him (perhaps even the forces of nature on Arrakis), and it is this balance between human control and ecological responsibility that Paul is able to strike so well. The quotation from the O. C. Bible only confirms this—Paul possesses the "senses" others (particularly the Harkonnens, the Emperor, the Spacing Guild) lack to appreciate the natural world surrounding him, seeing, hearing, and understanding what others cannot.

As this chapter has established Herbert's pattern of using language to sustain his ecocritical concerns, I would like to return to the dinner party the Atreides hosted upon their arrival in Arrakis as a more specific example of how Herbert encourages readers' participation in "ecological semantics." As this scene unfolds, Herbert blends language and ecology; according to Touponce, the episode is "nothing short of brilliant in the way it demonstrates the 'ecological semantics' of *Dune*, especially in the way in which utterances derive most of their meaning from the social context of communication in which they are produced and from paralinguistics."[110] Explaining "paralinguistics" as essentially nonverbal communication (such as "pauses, grunts, sighs, facial and body movements"),[111] Touponce identifies how Herbert uses metamessages throughout this scene. These frequently unconscious indicators of true meaning are not lost on Jessica, whose Bene Gesserit training monitors the flow and rhythm of the conversation (another of the book's musical qualities mentioned before). Touponce explains how Jessica, like Paul, demonstrates a level of complexity in linguistic choices that sets her apart as a more environmentally and linguistically sensitive character: "Despite the social context, Herbert controls in part our response to the passage through certain features of style. . . . [T]he lines devoted to [Jessica] are stylistically more complex. They amplify her thoughts as we go through the triad of modes from her simple emotional reaction to inwardly voiced hopes about Paul."[112] Jessica has become part of an ecological discourse, one that she must both participate in and interpret on several layers of identity, including mistress, mother, and Bene Gesserit. Through Jessica's intimate viewpoint of the banquet, readers are offered a perspective on the metamessages and paralinguistics that necessitates *their* participation, as well as Jessica's. It is through this participation that Herbert encourages a continued dialogue, a dialectical, a conversation between reader, author, and text.

Herbert stylistically sets off the characters' "interior monologues"—their thoughts and impressions, their secret fears, hopes, and desires—with italics, which typically informs the readers of an important insight to which they are about to be privy, reinforcing the sense of intimacy and participation that Herbert has fostered in his novel. Herbert does this throughout the dinner party, and this scene both draws the reader into a close personal connection with Jessica and also delineates how the characters themselves understand the important association between language, power, and the environment.

The banquet scene in particular exposes the nature of semantics and the role it plays in truth/deception, as Jessica remembers the lessons from her training at the skirts of the Reverend Mother Gaius Helen Mohiam:

> A thing to note about any espionage and/or counter-espionage school is the similar basic reaction pattern of all its graduates. Any enclosed discipline sets its stamp, its pattern, upon its students. That pattern is susceptible to analysis and prediction. Now, motivational patterns are going to be similar among all espionage agents. That is to say: there will be certain types of motivation that are similar despite differing schools or opposed aims. You will study first how to separate this element for your analysis—in the beginning, through interrogation patterns that betray the inner orientation of the interrogators; secondly, by close observation of language-thought orientation of those under analysis. You will find it fairly simple to determine the root languages of your subjects, of course, both through voice inflection and speech pattern.[113]

Jessica recalls verbatim the necessary skills to analyze and even manipulate those around her, a Bene Gesserit gift she uses to her advantage. But this lesson does more than just instruct her: it points to an overall strategy Herbert uses throughout his novel. He is perpetually mindful of how each element cannot be taken at face value alone. Even semantics have a personalized motivation behind them, and this motivation is the key for both the characters and the readers to understand and communicate with others. Herbert and his characters are consistently one step beyond the simple or expected: the author understands human psychology and motivation, and therefore he imbues his characters with this sense as well, particularly Paul and Jessica. This attention to his characters' understanding links back to *Dune*'s literary fugue: the key characters' perceptive natures distinguish them as ecoconscious beings, especially as Paul's motivation and understanding of semantics and language continually point to a deep appreciation of and concern for his environment and his ecological duties as leader, setting an example to *Dune*'s characters and readers alike.

The banquet scene also demonstrates a deeper examination of the Bene Gesserit gift of perception, through which they assess their environment and take appropriate action. As analyzed in chapter 3, Paul adopts the most healthful environmental relationship of the various characters; he also proves to be the most perceptive and "present" character, as demonstrated by his skills with Voice that Jessica and the Reverend Mother see so clearly by the novel's conclusion. But it is significant to note how the Bene Gesserit and, indeed, Paul come to develop this acute perception. Paul, ever the keen observer, understands the human necessity for a structure through which to view one's life: "The human requires a background grid through which to see his universe . . . ; focused consciousness by choice, this forms your grid."[114] For Paul, this structure is built with many distinct but interrelated segments: environment, language, ecological awareness, psychological understanding among them. His leadership necessitates a more intricate "grid" through which to operate, to perceive his ecological duties and identity within the universe. O'Reilly extrapolates on the Bene Gesserit mindset and how it relates to the author and his linguistic decisions: "Much of the Bene Gesserit technology of consciousness is based on the insights of general semantics. . . . The importance of general semantics in Herbert's work is twofold. First, it emphasized the importance of language and other cultural givens in providing a fundamental, *unconscious* structure for human thought and behavior; and second, it insisted that it was possible to *train* human beings into new semantic habits."[115] The metamessages, which those in control of the Voice are able to convey, work in both active and passive ways. Jessica's observational skills throughout the dinner party demonstrate part of the "grid" that Paul describes, and the scene is in line with the musical, rhythmic quality of Herbert's writing, while the event is centered around language (spoken and unspoken) and ecology. The layering of perception, language, and environment again encourages readers to create an ongoing relationship with the characters of *Dune*, with each rereading building upon the understanding one has gained with the previous reading.

The qualities of discourse and conversation that contribute to *Dune*'s unique qualities also epitomize the concerns Herbert himself had about interpersonal connections in the twentieth century.[116] By making his narrative interpersonal and participatory, Herbert has ensured that his novel *continues* to convey meaning and significance to contemporary readers. Touponce addresses this propensity for exchanges of ideas that Herbert valued:

> Indeed, he did not see his own work in *Dune* as a closed ideological system to be contemplated, but rather as something to be actively interpreted, transformed, parodied, exceeded, undermined, and subverted by later volumes in an open-ended dialogue. . . . As he saw mankind and its environment as part of a total situation, so also he saw in ecological terms that *Dune* was not an

aesthetic object to be contemplated, but rather each, reader and text, formed an ever-changing environment for the other during the act of reading.[117]

This interactive approach within Herbert's literature allows for an engaging experience that could potentially convey to readers the pervasive environmental interests that occupied the author, allowing them to form their own receptions and opinions of his works. Touponce confirms this in the beginning of his biography of Herbert, citing the author's intellectual background and ability to link a variety of discourses as paramount to the novel's success and longevity within both a science fiction and wider literary market.[118] Touponce's focus throughout the biography is the inseparable link between language and environment in *Dune*, or more specifically, discourse and ecology. Discourse presents yet another facet of language's influence throughout *Dune*.

While Touponce seems to advocate the dialogic nature of *Dune* as paramount to the other themes at work in the novel, he nevertheless recognizes that Paul encompasses a full understanding of ecology. He explains how he understands Herbert's work to present readers with an epitomized archetypal character, set in a classic "adventure plot," yet sensitive to the modern concerns of Herbert's culture:

> It is true that we can understand much of the hero's character and motivation from his family relationships, and Herbert tells us that he deliberately built into the novel oedipal structures and conflict. But Paul Atreides is also trained by nearly all of the social and political groups of the feudal and hierarchical world he inhabits, and he defines himself out of a dialogue with them and their ideologies. Therefore, plot in Herbert's *Dune* is absolutely devoid of any finalizing functions. Its goal is to place a person in various situations that expose and provoke him, to bring people together and make them collide in conflict—in such a way, however, that they do not remain within this area of plot-related contact but exceed its bounds. The real dialogical and ecological (they are practically the same thing in this novel) connections begin where the ordinary plot ends, having fulfilled its service function.[119]

Paul represents a truly relevant modern protagonist. He is continually engaged in a dialogue with the "ideologies" that have shaped him, but he does not allow his growth to be determined or terminated by his ideological background. Instead, he questions, transforms, opposes, and even rejects the hierarchies from which he comes and into which he journeys. He "changes the way" of the Fremen, denies the Bene Gesserit design for his life, and enters the realities that his prescient visions have only hinted at before, all with an autonomy and, at times, disillusionment, which speak so clearly to the contemporary reader. And most importantly, Paul and *Dune* offer readers a story of ecolinguistic complexity that set it and the Legendarium apart as works with unique ecological appeal:

> Ecology, therefore, has a much broader meaning than the mere study of organisms and their interaction with their environments. It can be globally social ecology, political ecology, economic ecology, and even language.... What *Dune* teaches us about language, whether used artistically or in everyday speech, is that both forms of utterance depend for their meaning on an ecological relationship between verbalized text and nonverbalized elements in their context.... One of the many achievements of *Dune* is the creation of an "ecology of the word" and ecological semantics.... Those characters in *Dune* who are capable of exploiting the capacity of words to mean different things in different social layers of their culture, such as Paul and Jessica Atreides, are ecologists in this broad sense.[120]

Touponce recognizes the pervasive quality of ecology and how Herbert would most certainly utilize all aspects of a given theme, creating a multifaceted composition of literary musicality, rhetoric, and discourse, pointing readers to how clearly defined Herbert has made his presentation of who has control of the planet's language and who is lacking in power and understanding.

In creating the Duniverse, Herbert has crafted his contemporary concerns inside a traditional framework, one in which the "adventure plot" common to so many works (including *The Lord of the Rings*) remains present and important to the structure of the novel, but which is ultimately eclipsed by the environmental theme and its significance. Even the adventure plot's presence has a more modern purpose behind its use: "Herbert really uses the adventure plot because it relies not so much on what the hero is, his social class and relationships, as in the realist novel, but more often on what he is not, on what (from the vantage point of the reality at hand) is unexpected and not predetermined.... [T]he adventure plot uses any stable social localization not as a finalizing real-life form but as a 'position' in a dialogue."[121] The dialogic nature of *Dune*'s plot structure reinforces Herbert's aim, bringing others to a recognition of the very real environmental crises facing them by engaging them in a participatory, communicative novel. A large part of the success of this engagement is due to Herbert's use of dialogue and discourse within *Dune*, and Touponce delineates three distinct types of discourse that the author employs. The first two, direct and indirect discourse, are typical of many narratives: there is direct communication or dialogue between characters, and there is the interior discourse of a character's inner thoughts, both of which have been addressed above. It is the third discourse, somewhat rarer in *Dune*, which has the greatest impact on the direct relationship between author, text, and audience.

The third type of discourse, what Touponce dubs "quasi-direct discourse,"[122] creates a direct link between the reader and the character who uses this quasi-direct discourse. According to Touponce, this is a deeply literary experience, something that can only occur in a textual setting (hence the "quasi" or partially apparent aspect of quasi-direct). In Touponce's opinion, this dialogic experience between reader and character is essential to the ecological nature of *Dune*, lending life and dynamism to the novel. He expounds on this form of discourse:

> Some linguists have called this mode "experienced speech" (*erlebte Rede*) on the analogy of listening to stage monologue in a play or trying to relate that experience to someone else. What the hero utters in the first person, a member of the audience experiences and relates in the third person. This transposition, occurring in the very depths of the experience of reception, stylistically aligns the experienced discourse with narrative. In brief, it is an aesthetic strategy for depicting the direct experience of another's speech, a form for conjuring up a living impression of that speech.[123]

Speech comes alive through this quasi-direct discourse, another way in which the language of *Dune* reflects the ever-present ecological disposition of Herbert and his literature. Just as the planet Arrakis has its own persona, the very language within the novel becomes its own being and presence, reaching out of the pages to influence and engage the audience on a temporal level.[124]

What the three modes of discourse accomplish is an *interaction*, the trait of any functioning ecosystem. Herbert layers these literary melodies of epic, myth, ecosystems, language, discourse, identity, power, and knowledge, all within the overarching theme of environment and its undeniable effect on Paul. By incorporating various discourses, Herbert has opened more avenues of conversation between his work, his readers, and even himself—his voice is present throughout *Dune*, as Touponce explains:

> When exploring the consciousness of a character, Herbert tries to create a smooth flow between these modes, so that we hardly notice that we have passed from skirting the depths of the unconscious to a level of conscious analysis.... Thus we can say that Herbert's authorial consciousness monitors and penetrates actively the consciousness of his characters. What is more, his own narrative voice, even when not presenting his consciousness, is often influenced and contaminated by the idioms of his characters.... Herbert never retains for himself an essential superiority of information. Instead, he keeps that indispensable minimum of pragmatic, purely informative omniscience necessary for the development of the plot.[125]

Herbert's chronicles are layered and complex, clearly favoring an ecological perspective, but one might also call it a human perspective, laying bare the interconnections between human culture and nature espoused by ecocritics. The author's interests are always in favor of what is healthy and beneficial for humanity, and one can easily argue that respecting and preserving one's environment is merely a part of this human well-being. Herbert's goal throughout the *Dune* chronicles is to continually bring awareness to the choices humanity makes on an individual and global scale, and how these choices have profound consequences within one's own world.

Ultimately, both authors have similar purposes in utilizing language to serve their environmental themes. Beyond world-building and myth-making, their use of language accentuates how important nature is, down to the very language and structures used to describe it. Further, language may even serve a moral purpose in their mythopoeic fantasies:

> They [the authors' intensions] help us see the ways in which mythopoeic fantasists express their understanding of our most basic desires to live a full life, see other people treated fairly, share in a good society, and experience the deepest human hopes for emancipation and happiness. They shield us from emotional and moral atrophy inherent in the dominant reductionist procedures of literary criticism which disconnects the aesthetic-cum-intellectual interest in a work of art from the endorsements of its author's opinion on what it means to live a human life. Finally, they point to the intimate tether-

ing of mythopoeic fantasy to general social concerns, including our current search for a new mythology of unified humanity.[126]

Tolkien and Herbert offer readers all of what Oziewicz claims above, especially "a new mythology of unified humanity," and their linguistic choices, no less than their ecocritical concerns and sacralization of nature, fortify their creation of stories, which offer a vision of unity, harmony, and joy achieved through a deeper and more meaningful relationship with our natural world.

CHAPTER 5

"TO HOLD COMMUNION WITH LIVING THINGS"

The Lives and Beliefs of Tolkien and Herbert

Humphrey Carpenter opens his biography of J. R. R. Tolkien with a note that Tolkien "did not entirely approve" of biography,[1] at least in terms of using it to interpret an author's literary output. In that same vein, this chapter is not attempting to use biography as a way to prove or disprove the claims that have already been made. Instead, I use details from Tolkien's and Herbert's lives and from their mythopoeic imaginations to shed light on what they believed was a better way to live as members of a shared global ecosystem. These biographical details might help to highlight what life events and inspirations "came to bear on Tolkien's" (and Herbert's) "imagination";[2] after all, their power of imagination is ultimately what brings readers back to their stories again and again and will endure. Through this chapter, readers will see how some of the authors' life events may have inspired their mythopoeic fiction, particularly themes of environment; how their spiritual beliefs impacted the literary worlds they built; and how passages in these literary worlds reveal these intersections between spirituality and environmentalism. In examining these details, readers may find inspiration in these authors' moral worldviews.

Both Tolkien and Herbert forged close bonds with nature early in their lives. In Tolkien's life, perhaps the most significant influences were his mother, the four years he lived in Sarehole, and his Catholic faith. Of course, there were others of importance (his love of language; his beloved wife, Edith; his time serving in World War I; the bonds of friendship he created with the Inklings), but these formative influences seem to have left an indelible mark on Tolkien's life and on his writings. Tolkien's days in the English countryside provided rich fuel for his imagination, as he and his brother Hilary went on adventures through a landscape that sounds much like the Shire;[3] indeed, Tolkien later admitted that Sarehole became the inspiration for the Shire and Hobbits.[4] After his earliest years of poor health and family instability in South Africa and later the tragedy of his mother's death, Sarehole was also the landscape in which he was perhaps most happy and at peace: "Sarehole was Tolkien's vision of 'a kind of lost paradise.' He once said that he had a 'strange sense of coming home' when at the age of three he first arrived in the Warwickshire village. Sarehole had 'good Waterstones and elm trees and small quiet rivers.' It was surrounded by open fields and farmlands, though in the distance one could see the grimy smoke of nearby Birmingham."[5] His time here must also have influenced his love of trees, which would become so important in his literature as well. Before the age of ten, Tolkien had become a firm tree friend: "And though he liked drawing trees he liked most of all to be *with* trees. He would climb them, lean against them, even talk to them. It saddened him to discover that not everyone shared his feelings towards them."[6] His relationship with nature took on almost religious significance: "Frequent long walks around the countryside—a practice established and encouraged by his mother—instilled in him a deep, almost reverent love of nature. Sarehole was undisturbed by factories, motor cars, suburban subdivisions, and social upheavals; it was an idyllic setting in which to grow up."[7] The trees, plants, and people alike lent an "idyllic" quality to his youth, one that, while not destined to last, never left his creative imagination: "'I could draw you a map of every inch,'" Tolkien said when he was seventy-four years old. 'I loved it with an intensity of love that was a kind of nostalgia reversed.'"[8] Clearly, the beauties and joys of a close relationship with nature that Tolkien writes about in his letters and his Legendarium have been drawn from profound personal experience.

Similarly, Herbert had a childhood that was a mix of joy and tragedy; he had a difficult relationship with his stern father, and both parents were "on-again, off-again alcoholics" during his youth,[9] but young Frank found solace in nature: "He spent much of his time away from the house, fishing, hunting, and hiking. To a large degree he grew up on his own and became independent at an early age. Young Frank become something of a provider for the family, as he brought home trout, salmon, crabs, clams, rabbits and grouse for the supper table."[10] These early experiences in the natural world left a lasting impact on Herbert, providing him with "independence" as well as an appreciation of the lands in 1930s Washington state. His childhood experiences also found their way into his writings, as Tolkien's did, with ecology emerging as one of the most important themes in his fiction as well as a lifelong interest and political cause. Perhaps it is not surprising, then, that both writers craft environmental concerns so carefully into their mythopoeic fantasies, framing them as important a part of their world-building as any other element.

From their early experiences in nature, both authors take up an ethical model of environmental care, that of stewardship, as well as decrying industrialization, urbanization, pollution, or other forms of careless environmental impact. Much of Tolkien's ethical framework derived from his Catholicism; he believed "'that the natural world was a gift from God and that man was obligated to act as its steward.'"[11] Jeffers and other scholars have acknowledged stewardship's contemporary negative connotations, that it can be used as possible justification for the exploitation of nature, but Tolkien's view of it instead fits the idea of "servanthood stewardship," which "'not only sees the intrinsic value of creation but also conceives of humans as servants within it.'"[12] Respect becomes a key underlying value in this model as servanthood stewardship "is based on the recognition that the environment has worth in and of itself, and that people who inhabit the Earth are just taking care of it for a short time before passing it on to others."[13] As I asserted in previous chapters, communities like the Hobbits' live out this form of servanthood stewardship, becoming an extension of "sacrificial humility," which is "expressed broadly in terms of the preservation of people's lives and freedoms and more narrowly, but perhaps even more fundamentally, in terms of the protection of the natural environment in the landscapes of ... Middle-earth."[14] Thus, via Tolkien's invented characters, readers are presented with models of "sacrificial humility" (more secular language here might be "decentering anthropocentric attitudes") as valuable for the quality of human life as well as beneficial for environmental relationships.

These values are mirrored in Tolkien's writings as well. Earlier chapters acknowledged stewardship as an important environmental model offered through the Legendarium; this model and the pressing need for activism are among the final images with which Tolkien leaves readers. Tolkien impresses upon us how important restorative, healing action is for Middle-earth and for perhaps our own world. For example, the work of renewal begins almost immediately after Sauron is overthrown. As Aragorn travels back to Minas Tirith to claim his crown, readers see the work of healing: "Then all others that dwelt afar went back to their homes rejoicing; but in the City there was labour of many willing hands to rebuild and renew and to remove all the scars of war and the memory of the darkness."[15] Even the King himself is not exempt from this work. Gandalf entrusts him and the people of Gondor with their own labor (also showing Gandalf's strengths as a steward himself): "It is your task to order its beginning and to preserve what may be preserved. For though much has been saved, much must now pass away."[16] As readers travel from Gondor to Isengard, here too creatures are occupied in rebuilding their environments: "They rode to Isengard, and saw how the Ents had busied themselves. All the stone-circle had been thrown down and removed, and the land within was made into a garden filled with orchards and trees, and a stream ran through it; but in the midst of all there was a lake of clear water, and out of it the Tower of Orthanc rose still, tall and impregnable, and its black rock was mirrored in the pool."[17] A former place of slavery and death has been transformed with a garden and orchard. The symbolism of the two versions of Isengard could not be more different. Everywhere in Middle-earth, people are trying to counter the evil effects of Sauron's reach, and it seems fitting that we return to the Shire not as the idyllic place we left it but as the site of an environmental battle. As Gildor has reminded Frodo, the Hobbits do not own the land but are instead stewards, and here they must come into their rightful roles as stewards and caretakers of the land they have been entrusted. Tolkien writes these passages with an emotional rawness: "It was one of the saddest hours in their lives. . . . [Sam] pointed to where the tree had stood under which Bilbo had made his Farewell Speech. It was lying lopped and dead in the field. As if this was the last straw Sam burst into tears."[18] Many readers have grown to love and empathize with Sam through his journey in the trilogy, and to see him in this vulnerable moment, weeping for the death of a tree like he might the death of a friend—it is a powerful narrative moment. Yes, Sam is mourning the memories tied to the Party Tree, but he is also genuinely grieved by this tree's death. The lonely image of the tree "lying lopped and dead in the field" drives home the value Sam and the Hobbits attach to every part of their environment.[19] This destruction is the motivation they need to come into their roles as protectors and caretakers of the Shire.

Tolkien, though, does not end the story with these sad images. Instead, the Hobbits are roused to work, to labor to bring about the beautiful landscape they have lost. Because of Sam's efforts as faithful steward, the Shire is rewarded:

> Spring surpassed his wildest hopes. His trees began to sprout and grow, as if time was in a hurry and wished to make one year do for twenty.... Altogether 1420 in the Shire was a marvelous year. Not only was there wonderful sunshine and delicious rain, in due times and perfect measure, but there seemed something more: an air of richness and growth, and a gleam of a beauty beyond that of mortal summers that flicker and pass upon this Middle-earth... And no one was ill, and everyone was pleased, except those who had to mow the grass.[20]

Here Tolkien has given us a triumphant catalog of the most "marvelous year" in the Shire's recent history, with all things thriving and growing and happiness abounding, but we are reminded that work is still needed, even in the most mundane, very human tasks, like mowing the lawn.

Yet, even this joy is not without loss. For various reasons, Frodo cannot stay; the Shire has not been saved for him. The wounded hero, the self-abnegating peacemaker, Frodo exemplifies the bittersweet loss that permeates much of Tolkien's writings, perhaps representative of Sarehole's irrevocable transformation, or the loss of so many of his friends in World War I: "'It must often be so, Sam, when things are in danger: some one has to give them up, lose them, so that others may keep them.... [You will be] the most famous gardener in history... and keep alive the memory of the age that is gone, so that people will remember the Great Danger and so love their beloved land all the more.'"[21] Earlier chapters have framed Sam as a hero of Middle-earth of as much significance as Frodo. In general, it is not so important to prove one more heroic than the other, but in terms of an ecocritical reading of these books, the characters' choices *are* important. If Sam is truly heroic, then part of his heroism is in rebuilding the Shire, of being willing to do the hard work needed to steward the land through his generation and into the next. He stands as perhaps the best model of environmental care that Tolkien has given us. Frodo, however, cannot persevere in his current state. He has to leave behind his own lands to find peace and healing. This action could be characterized as an abandoning of hope, or at least of the hope the Shire offers him. (Though, as Jeffers explains, his sacrificial actions have their own merits.) Frodo's decision to leave is not necessarily wrong, but Sam sustains hope to the last, never abandoning his responsibilities to his fellow Hobbits or his beloved Shire. Frodo is undeniably heroic, but Sam also models heroism as honest, unassuming, and humble, someone who is willing to do the work needed to ensure long-term success and growth, to help his land thrive and be a place of beauty, use, and renewal. Also like Frodo, Sam is a selfless hero—a good steward, taking care of what does not truly belong to him until the next person or people can carry on the work of stewardship, and so forth. From a mythopoeic framework, invoking the three functions of fantasy, readers can recover a vision of their own environmental relationships by Sam's example; they can escape into a better world, peopled with heroes like Sam; and they can be consoled by the beautiful, joyous Eucatastrophe of *The Return of the King*, renewing hope and faith in the "gifts" of the natural world.

Tolkien tells his readers that work will be needed to reach this kinship, and this is an important part of Tolkien's environmental vision. The people of Middle-earth cannot accomplish healing and renewal without hard work, and ecocritical readers must also feel a need to engage in this work. Gandalf cares that there will be a clean, whole land to leave people, even if it won't last forever: "'Other evils there are that may come; for Sauron is himself but a servant or emissary. Yet it is not our part to master all the tides of the world, but to do what is in us for the succor of those years wherein we are set, uprooting the evil in the fields that we know, so that those who live after may have clean earth to till. What weather they shall have is not ours to rule.'"[22] Gandalf repeats this message throughout the trilogy, to make good and productive use of the time we have, and our relationship to our environment is no exception. Gandalf wants to preserve the ecosystem, so to speak, even at cost and sacrifice to the individual (Tolkien's theme of self-abnegation emerges again). He recognizes the importance of an environmental balance—to offset the damage that has been done with good work. Here he embodies a true steward, someone who is generous and puts the needs of others before himself. Gandalf recognizes the peril and potential failure he faces, but, like Sam, he sustains hope and urges perseverance: "'We must walk open-eyed into that trap, with courage, but small hope for ourselves. For, my lords, it may well prove that we ourselves shall perish utterly in a black battle far from the living lands; so that even if Barad-dur be thrown down, we shall not live to see a new age. But this, I deem, is our duty. And better so than to perish nonetheless—as we surely shall, if we sit here—and know as we die that no new age shall be.'"[23] If readers are to look to Gandalf as a better example of stewardship (a kind of escape into a better version of what they already know), then his and the Fellowship's ultimate success provides an even more enriching consolation. The "happy ending" we will see later is not trite or unearned. Instead, Gandalf's "small hope" and sense of "duty" are rewarded because he was faithful in sustaining hope and carrying out duty. Readers, too, can experience the joy of the trilogy's resolution, and readers, too, can feel the hope and duty laid on us to love, appreciate, and preserve what is "good" in our own world.

Tolkien's presentation of stewardship is multifaceted. Denethor is a literal steward of Gondor, awaiting the return of Aragorn the king but also resenting that his own line cannot claim leadership. We can contrast this role with someone like Tom Bombadil, or Sam: though not a steward in the formal sense, we see Tom has true authority (he is "Master") because he loves his dominion, caring for it and respecting it. Sam, too, takes some measure of control in reshaping the Shire, but he does so out of a simple love for nature in its own right, without an ulterior, personal motive. These two models promote life, health, and growth, even in the face of Middle-earth's crises. Denethor's twisted idea of stewardship, however, perpetuates decay, though there is still a message of hope, symbolized by the White Tree. This natural image underscores what Aragorn's return truly means—the healing of an ecosystem, both its people and its lands, both equally valuable and necessary. As readers see, Denethor's selfish desire for personal glory leads to needless loss of life. He does not value Gondor for its own sake, as it is. He instead dwells on the past, obsessing over what was instead of what can be, willing to sacrifice what good things are left in Minas Tirith rather than relinquish power: "'I would have things as they were in all the days of my life . . . and in the days of my longfathers before me: to be the Lord of this City in peace, and leave my chair to a son after me, who would be his own master and no wizard's pupil. But if doom denies this to me then I will have *naught*: neither life diminished, nor love halved, nor honour abated.'"[24] Gandalf's fitting reply shows his much deeper and more mature understanding of what it means to be a steward: "'To me it would not seem that a Steward who faithfully surrenders his charge is diminished in love or in honour.'"[25] It is only through the more charitable, environmentally healthful model of good stewardship that Gandalf and others embody that Middle-earth can have the flourishing growth it needs.[26] Further, through escape, we can see the value of these fictional models in our own world, a vision of how stewardship can build a better, more healthful future.

Herbert also believed in stewardship as an essential act of ethical environmental care. To illustrate his father's commitment to environmental caretaking, Brian Herbert writes of a piece of driftwood that Frank had used as a desktop for a number of years: "Before we moved again in 1955, Dad returned the driftwood desktop slab to the beach. He told my mother he had been the custodian of the wood for a short time. Years later he would say something similar to me, that none of us ever 'own' land. We are merely caretakers of it, passing it along one day to other caretakers. It is this way with the Earth, he said. We are stewards of it, not owners, and one day future generations will assume the responsibility."[27] Herbert's Duniverse models stewardship, too, as generations of Atreides and Fremen care for their planet, albeit in sometimes imperfect ways, but always with an intension of handing off a better version to the next generation. However, both authors condemn activities that would lessen the health and diversity of the environment, especially their homes.

While Tolkien was not necessarily involved in formal protest movements, many of his statements about England's beauty and the impact of industrialization place him within the ideological realm of these movements. According to Veldman, Tolkien "'protested against the basic assumptions of industrial Britain'" and "'denounced the exaltation of mechanization and the narrow definition of economic progress that resulted in the degradation of the natural environment.'"[28] "Industrial Britain" and "exaltation of mechanization" came literally close to home, as the early 1900s saw much industrialization and urbanization of formerly rural areas, including Sarehole: "With an ever-increasing population, the surrounding villages eventually became the city's suburbs and, ultimately, became completely absorbed into the metropolis itself. This was the fate of Sarehole, and Tolkien was saddened as he saw the steady encroachments of civilization marching towards the countryside in the form of new houses, factories, and suburban railways."[29] It is no wonder, then, that the Shire, emblematic of Tolkien's idealized childhood, becomes the battleground for industrialized power on the one hand (Sharkey's hideous transformation of the Hobbits' home) and environmental reclamation on the other (the "Golden Age" of harvest and plenty that follows the Scouring of the Shire). Though Tolkien recognized that Sarehole and the Shire would never be quite the same as they once were, the ending of *The Lord of the Rings* allows a small measure of victory over the forces of industry.

Herbert, too, saw the effects of environmental change and harm and made it his mission to do something, both creatively and personally: "Dad was a daily witness to conditions in Tacoma, which in the 1950s was known as one of the nation's most polluted cities, largely due to a huge smelter whose stack was visible from all over the city, a stack that belched filth into the sky. The air was 'so thick you could chew it,' my father liked to quip. The increasing pollution he saw all around him, in the city of his birth, contributed to his resolve that something had to be done to save the Earth. This became, perhaps, the most important message of *Dune*."[30] In his own life, Herbert educated others on the importance of environmental care and oversaw many of his own environmental "projects," aimed at finding more efficient and environmentally friendly farming methods, land use, and energy sources. For his job as a senator's speechwriter, Herbert was exposed to an enormous variety of topics, especially those of environmental import. Among his research topics were "tideland oils, the Submerged Lands Acts, the Continental Shelf Lands Acts, land grants, an 'oil-for-education' congressional amendment, Federal Aid to Education, issues of grazing on national forest lands, and the highly publicized Hells Canyon issue involving construction of a huge hydroelectric project on the Snake River."[31] Clearly, Herbert had a well-filled political-ecological education and would sometimes draft senate bills; in other words, he had one foot in the political-activist world, and the other in the literary world. In a different way, Herbert spread environmental awareness through his Duniverse, as each work presents issues of resource scarcity, pollution, and industrialization at the core of the planet's fate and the characters' moral decisions. Herbert drew inspiration from the real-life crises he saw around him: "From an early stage of his writing, Frank Herbert was tuned-in to the problem of finite resources on this planet. At a time of increasing and wasteful consumer consumption in the United States, he saw, quite accurately, that it could not last forever."[32] Such models of "wasteful consumer consumption" find their way into both Herbert's and Tolkien's created worlds, and it is clear that these authors want readers to be as equally disturbed by such consequences as they and their characters are. (The work of environmental reclamation and stewardship is present in their fiction as inspiration for readers to draw from as well.)

Another parallel between these authors' lives is in their spiritual beliefs. Tolkien's devotion to Catholicism held a significant place in his life, even if his literary creations did not adopt overtly Catholic "messages." Yet, from his letters and conversations with others, it is clear that his faith was an inseparable part of his identity and his worldview, shaping the ethics of his imagined worlds as much as of his own existence. One of the reasons for religious devotion must be his mother: "Indeed it might be said that after she died his religion took the place in his affections that she had previously occupied. The consolation that it provided was emotional as well as spiritual."[33] Tolkien's Catholic values manifest themselves in various ways in his mythopoeic fantasies, especially in how he portrays his characters' relationships with the land and each other. As readers have seen, servanthood stewardship and self-sacrifice are pivotal to the quest's success in *The Lord of the Rings*, as are other virtues, such as compassion, charity, and courage. Tolkien's idea of stewardship, especially, evokes a sense of Christian morality, as Dickerson and Evans describe it as a "heartfelt devotion to a particular place and the people who live there; sacrificial willingness to do what is necessary to protect and preserve it. These are necessary agrarian attitudes, and they are Christian virtues."[34] Much scholarship has already analyzed the moral choices of the Legendarium's characters; what is more important in this chapter is a recognition that Tolkien's spirituality informs his mythopoeic fantasy, as does Herbert's.

Herbert's faith, however, is perhaps harder to pin down (his son claimed that it might be "impossible . . . to categorize Frank Herbert's religious beliefs"),[35] though he too defined himself as a spiritual man: "He ascribed to no single organized belief system, but instead drew from many. He was attracted to Zen Buddhism in particular, as can be seen in his classic novel, *Dune*, where there are wordless truths and 'Zensunni' and 'Zensufi' belief systems."[36] Zen Buddhism appealed to Herbert particularly because it "is a highly ethical belief system, . . . hold[s] a spiritual reverence for nature and for the preservation of life on this planet,"[37] and is perhaps more accepting of other religious and philosophical beliefs,[38] all extremely important attributes for Herbert. Among the important spiritual influences from which Herbert drew were the Coast Salish Indians' religious beliefs, which he "would come to know and respect";[39] he also "admired the link between Native Americans and their environment, the way they lived for centuries in harmony with nature, not wreaking havoc upon it as the white man did."[40] As a result of studying these beliefs and befriending members of the Coast Salish Indian tribe, Herbert "developed a deep respect for the natural rhythms of nature. The ecology message, so prevalent in much of his writing, is one of his most important legacies."[41] Herbert's spiritual influences helped guide his ethical decision-making throughout his life and reinforced his deep love and respect for nature. Ultimately, his son saw him as a highly moral man, devoted to the truth in all circumstances: "He was basically a man of faith, and this made him good and true and strong."[42]

Like Tolkien's, Herbert's literary works are testament to the values he held closest, as his son remarks: "His deep commitment to ethics and the survival of humanity were apparent through his writings. He believed in quality of life, not merely in scraping by, and he spoke deftly (and at times didactically) about this through his characters."[43] As much as Herbert saw Western culture and white men in particular as destructive environmental forces, his devotion was always to "the survival of humanity" as inherently valuable, and he saw the caretaking of nature as a contribution to humans' "quality of life." In order to convey these values, he began collecting ideas that would later form the Duniverse, set on a distant planet but with fully human concerns: "borrowing from the American Indian's opinion of white culture, he would describe how man inflicts himself upon his environment, usurping it and failing to live in harmony with it."[44] This format worked because it "demonstrates effectively with the simplified ecology of the planet Arrakis how important and surprising the connections among things in an ecosystem can be,"[45] and "Herbert also uses the cognitive estrangement of an alien planet and its indigenous people to unwrap for his readers some aspects of the relationship between nature and culture."[46] Thus, Herbert combines his own ecological concerns with his spiritual beliefs, that interconnections between people and ecosystems are present in our real world as much as in Arrakis, and that human culture has a profound impact on nature (both key tenets in ecocriticism).

    Finally, the Zen writings of Alan W. Watts also served as inspiration for Herbert's beliefs and literature; Watts describes a "paradox in which the abandonment of safe courses of action opened a person to ineffable spiritual truths that could not otherwise be attained."[47] Important to Herbert's mythopoeic fantasy are the ideas of change, balance, and harmony (ideas that I would assert are also significant to Tolkien's mythopoeic works). Herbert shared Watts's belief in insecurity as a means of balance, as "the natural state of equilibrium in the universe was not a stable, fixed point or condition of being."[48] Rather, its natural state is one of dynamism: "It was instead a changing thing, always presenting new faces and new experiences. For an individual to be in harmony with the universe, my father believed, he needed to place himself in synchronization with the changing state of nature and human society. He needed to take risks. Thus in many of his stories he stressed the importance of adaptability, and his characters often had to adjust in order to survive."[49] As readers will see, Paul Atreides and his descendants frequently urge balance and "adaptability" as solutions to the sometimes radical changes of the planet, its culture, and humanity itself. Such characteristics are symptoms of a healthy ecosystem as much as they are of Herbert's fictional stories, thus revealing another way in which spirituality and environmentalism are intertwined in these authors' mythopoeic creations.

The *Dune* sequels, especially, pick up these themes. In *Dune Messiah*, Paul speaks to Stilgar, the faithful Fremen leader, about this need for adaptability and balance: "'Stilgar,' Paul said, 'you urgently need a sense of balance which can come only from an understanding of long-term effects.'"[50] In another conversation with his Tleilaxu servant, Bijaz, Paul contemplates these same ideas: "'I have heard the Bene Gesserit say,' Bijaz said, 'that there is nothing firm, nothing balanced, nothing durable in all the universe—that nothing remains in its state, that each day, sometimes each hour, brings change.'"[51] Paul's son, Leto II, sees the connection between balance and nature as he gains awareness of how the planet's ecological transformation has perhaps compromised the original beauty and power of the desert: "'We've been very one-sided about Arrakis,' he said. 'Barbaric of us. There's a certain momentum in what we've been doing, but now we must undo some of our work. The scales must be brought into better balance.'"[52] His word choices reinforce images of balance: his and the Fremen's "one-sided" actions, the "scales" that must equalize. Leto continues to use distinctive imagery in describing his relationship with nature: "'My vision,' he said. 'Unless we restore the dance of life here on Dune, the dragon on the floor of the desert will be no more.'"[53] While Leto's remarks are practical (without the desert, there will be no more sandworms, "the dragon on the floor of the desert"), they are also evocative of Herbert's ecocritical and spiritual concerns. Herbert desired humans to "restore the dance of life" on their own planet, finding the "rhythms of nature" that Kynes did not and restoring balance between the human and nonhuman worlds. Herbert's mythopoeic fantasy reinforces his real-life values and encourages readers to apprehend nature as more than a passive object. Like Tolkien's depictions of stewardship and restorative action, Herbert's Duniverse implies a need for activism to achieve the equilibrium Leto envisions for right relations with the environment. Thus, each author in his own way encourages readers to see action as a necessary solution to our current disconnect with the created world.

Tolkien and Herbert's cultural contexts, too, shaped their writings. In Tolkien's own life, the industrialism of the early 1900s and World War I were forces that influenced his and many others' vision of the modern world. The large-scale consumerism of post–World War II America led into many of the cultural shifts of the 1960s, influencing the themes in Herbert's writings, too: "*Dune* is imbued with references extrapolated from life in the sixties, some of them introduced deliberately . . . others . . . unconsciously. It is in fact easy to find parallels in the major conflicts at work in *Dune* and in the ones that were upsetting the America of that decade."[54] Among some of the "major conflicts at work in *Dune*" and 1960s America was the same root problem, perhaps, as in World War I Britain—the uses of power. In their personal lives and in their mythopoeic fantasies, both authors are skeptical of those who would use power to gain success, especially technological or organizational power. Tolkien's Legendarium repeatedly promotes cooperation as a means of creating success over hierarchical power, the "power with" model that Jeffers writes of: "Tolkien's work advocates partnership between people and the environment, whether in the wilderness or in cultivated spaces."[55] Herbert's works, too, challenge those in positions of power, even to the point of questioning (and later dismantling) his heroes: "Paul and Leto are the fallible leaders with immense power, aware of the fact that, while they must respond to their calling as leaders, whatever they do or fail to do the effects, because of their immense powers, will no longer be local and controllable."[56] As his son notes, hierarchical power is at the heart of the Duniverse's concerns: "Heroes are dangerous, especially when people follow them slavishly, treating them like gods."[57] In *Children of Dune,* for example, power is called into question as a force that corrupts and therefore requires adaptability. Leto II recognizes the limits of power, and how the Atreides and their Fremen citizens need to rule with fairness: "'One uses power by grasping it lightly. To grasp too strongly is to be taken over by power, and thus to become its victim.'"[58] Like Tolkien, Herbert berates systems of power that "take over" others, especially those who are in vulnerable positions. And nature is among the most vulnerable victims in current society, one that needs the restorative activism of concerned individuals to be its voice and protectors against the violence of irresponsible power.

Indeed, Herbert saw violence as profoundly detrimental to human and environmental cooperation. Like Frodo at the end of *The Lord of the Rings,* Herbert was a sensitive, peaceful man, not deriving pleasure from others' pain, even if the "other" was nonhuman: "During the Depression when he had to hunt to put food on the table, he felt remorse each time he shot game. It was a philosophy of non-violence that would ultimately lead to his involvement in the movement to stop the war in Vietnam. His anti-war beliefs were directly linked to his ecological writings. . . . Wars were devastating not only to people, but in the harm they inflicted upon the environment."[59] What emerges from Herbert's "philosophy of non-violence" is an emphasis on collective ethical responsibility and, even more so, the personal obligation to take action against hierarchical power, corruption, and, of course, environmental degradation. Tolkien's own attitudes toward violence and hierarchical power appear similarly aligned with Herbert's. While not perhaps a strict pacifist (he served in World War I), Tolkien had his reservations about systems of political power: "Tolkien noted in 1943 that 'My political opinions lean more and more to Anarchy (philosophically understood, meaning abolition of control, not whiskered men with bombs)—or to "unconstitutional" Monarchy.'"[60] His desire for "abolition of control" corresponds to Herbert's attitudes toward overly powerful leaders and systems. Further, in his letters to his son Christopher, who served in World War II, Tolkien shares his own experiences in using writing to find solace from the horrors of war (*Letters*, 78). These letters suggest that Tolkien, too, saw a measure of senseless violence and harm that results from war, whether such war is "moral" or not.

Neither Tolkien's Legendarium nor Herbert's Duniverse offers a simple solution to such problems; in fact, each entry in the *Dune* series seems to raise more questions about the feasibility of balancing the needs of a modern and fallible society with those of nature. Even the first novel complicates the issue of healthful environmental relationships: "*Dune* even goes so far as to question whether embedded practice, or living deliberatively as part of nature, is possible given both the difficulty of finding today the 'nature' of which we are a part and of negotiating the imposed burdens we face in the shadow of a spatially and psychologically imperializing political economy."[61] Herbert, for one, saw completely "embedded practice" as a myth, that no family could live entirely "off the grid" and free from modern conveniences,[62] and certainly not with the "imposed burdens" of a "spatially and psychologically imperializing political economy" that Otto references. Nevertheless, Herbert was also an optimist at heart, using his considerable energies to improve upon his environment to the best of his abilities, "deliberatively" drawing "power with" the land and adopting as positive an environmental relationship as he could.

Both authors did indeed believe in hope and optimism, and that regular people have the potential to create important change. In their literature, especially, ordinary characters are presented with many moral decisions, great and small, and such scenes suggest a larger point—that the behavior of everyone, no matter their position in society, is significant. For example, in the third *Dune* novel, Paul (now the blind "Preacher") asserts, "'It is not always the majestic concerns of Imperial ministers which dictate the course of history, nor is it necessarily the pontifications of priests which move the hands of God.'"[63] The everyday citizen can "dictate the course of history" and "move the hands of God." Other textual examples reinforce this theme, as well. One of the chapter's epigraphs asserts that no matter what progress is made in human civilization, *"the very future of humankind, depends on the relatively simple actions of single individuals."*[64] The Hobbits, too, exhibit this idea that "relatively simple actions of single individuals" (Frodo's decision to carry the Ring; Sam's unfaltering loyalty and service to Frodo and his cause; even earlier, Bilbo's moment of courage in going down the tunnel to Smaug or, more profoundly, his mercy in sparing Gollum's life) have an enormous impact on the future of their homes and of Middle-earth itself.

In their literary and cultural impacts, Tolkien and Herbert are distinctive. In light of the qualities this study has identified, it should not be surprising that many readers and critics have drawn comparisons between their "epic" literary creations. However, I would add that some of the themes and values they promote in their mythopoeic fantasies do find analogues in other modern and postmodern works.[65] Amid Tolkien's contemporaries, certainly C. S. Lewis and Charles Williams emerge as writers with many of the same religious undertones to their writings (and Lewis arguably advocates for more healthful environmental relationships). Lewis, of course, upholds humble courage in the face of enormous evil, self-sacrifice, and servant-stewardship. Williams's themes of exchange, coinherence, and redemption find parallels in both Tolkien's and Herbert's fiction, particularly in how each presents the presence of the divine in humanity and in nature. Perhaps a less obvious parallel, James Hilton's 1933 novel *Lost Horizon* arguably echoes Tolkien's particular concern with the demands of time—to use it responsibly, to value the quality of our time on Earth rather than quantity, to measure time and success in terms of our interpersonal and ecological relationships rather than our material possessions. Finally, Flannery O'Connor's 1950s and 1960s literary output raises similar themes as Tolkien's and Herbert's, and like these men, she was quite spiritual. Her works posit belief in a transcendent and merciful God as valuable, one that exposes the hypocrisy of many of her characters' lives and also enriches their relationships (with God and with others). O'Connor, too, meditates on themes of time, redemption, and even environmentalism, while values of compassion and empathy frequently emerge from her stories. In fact, like Tolkien's and Herbert's fantasies, O'Connor's writings offer readers a profound reading experience both in light of and separate from her religious convictions; each story presents fundamentally human crises and decisions, highlighting how the smallest and greatest individual decisions can have wide-reaching and moral consequences, thus potentially stirring readers to reevaluate their own participation in their human and nonhuman world. In drawing attention to these works, I acknowledge that Tolkien's and Herbert's mythopoeic fantasy literature are just one part of a large collection of works from various genres and writers in the twentieth century that interrogate similar questions and promote ecocritical consciousness. However, these two authors have done so in distinctive ways and with a cultural impact greater than perhaps any other (mythopoeic) texts.

I would like to leave this chapter with two images that perhaps best encapsulate the lives and beliefs of these two extraordinary authors. First, there is Brian Herbert's description of his father:

> My father once told me he felt he was most like the Fremen leader, Stilgar. This surprised me until I realized that Stilgar was the equivalent of a Native American leader in the story—a person who defended time-honored ways that did not harm the ecology of the planet. Stilgar was an outdoors man like my father, a person more comfortable in the wild reaches of the planet than its more "civilized" enclaves. Such a strong name, Stilgar, combining the phonetic elements of "steel" and "guard." He was the stalwart and determined guardian of Dune, a position not dissimilar from the one my father placed himself in with respect to Earth.[66]

Maybe Stilgar did not reach the same heights of talent, power, and glory as Paul, but he was indeed the "stalwart and determined guardian of Dune," an honorable and admirable role that Herbert imbued in his own life. Tolkien too described himself in terms of his literary inventions; writing in an unsent letter, Tolkien says this about himself: "I am in fact a *Hobbit* (in all but size). I like gardens, trees and unmechanized farmlands; I smoke a pipe, and like good plain food (unrefrigerated), but detest French cooking; I like, and even dare to wear in these dull days, ornamental waistcoats. I am fond of mushrooms (out of a field); have a very simple sense of humour (which even my appreciative critics find tiresome); I go to bed late and get up late (when possible). I do not travel much."[67] Tolkien's honest and self-deprecating depiction of himself is humorous, but it also reveals the sweet, simple desires of his own life for the same things that Hobbits value: gardens, good food, a closeness to home and to nature—in short, quality of life above power and consumption. While not as obviously an ecoguardian by nature as Herbert, perhaps, Tolkien would no doubt surprise others as his Hobbits did if the need arose. I have no doubt that each author loved his environment and his fellow humankind; I believe this love endures in the Legendarium and Duniverse.

CONCLUSION

As this book has acknowledged, "epic" is the most common comparison drawn between Tolkien's Legendarium and Herbert's Duniverse. The previous five chapters have uncovered several reasons why these two bodies of work should be put in conversation with each other; however, "epic" is an equally valid classification for these fantasies. There are certainly some overlaps between the labels for epics, myths, and mythopoeic works, and so it is fitting that these categories are used to describe Tolkien's and Herbert's works. M. H. Abrams notes that the label *epic* can reach beyond the traditional, Homeric criteria and "is often applied, by extension, to works which differ in many respects from this model but manifest the epic spirit in the scale, the scope, and the profound human importance of their subjects."[1] Marxist critic George Lukács adds a more comprehensive definition of *epic*, broadening this category to include the "bourgeois epic" for any novels that "reflect social reality on a broad scale."[2] This broader definition clarifies how Tolkien's and Herbert's mythopoeic fiction operate as epic works (a phrase that in the past has been loosely applied to them because of their grand "scale") in, most importantly, "the profound human importance of their subjects." Thus, epic works do more than follow Homeric or other criteria: they demonstrate how their authors have synthesized a multitude of social, cultural, religious, and political ideologies and then presented these ideologies in a way that elicits an impactful response from their audience.

My contention throughout this study is that Tolkien's and Herbert's emphasis on the environment is part of what qualifies their books as unique and valuable, particularly in terms of the specific "social reality" that they are mirroring. I also see the environment as a crucial unifying theme. *The Lord of the Rings* is not simply a modern epic, a high fantasy work, or a classic story of good and evil, selfishness and sacrifice, bravery and heroism in the face of powers greater than oneself; likewise, *Dune* is not simply science fiction, or a liminal work that blurs the lines between science fiction and fantasy, or a reflection on the dangers of a superhero. They are indeed all these things. But my analysis has identified certain central ecocritical themes that unite these various constituents and provide meaning to these works. In my research, the essential element tying together all these aspects has been the environment, and I believe it is worth examining in its various depictions, all of which apply to these novels in different and important ways. Thus, while *epic* is appropriate to describe these works, the previous chapters have illuminated how important the environment is in supporting the other significant aspects of the Legendarium and Duniverse.

As chapter 1 began with a conversation about mythopoeic fantasy, I would like to return to it, though this time in consideration of what mythic legacy these writers leave behind for their readers. Both authors' fantasies do provide a mythic "feeling" to their works, over and above the fact that they are mythopoeic works. The Legendarium and Duniverse give readers a sense that their worlds exist outside of even the novels themselves:

> As with Tolkien, [Herbert's] reader has the impression that the story he is reading does not start on the first page but exists beyond the book and extends backwards to the past, our immediate future. The effects for the readers are both an expansion of his imagination (wondering what may not have been told by the author) and a strengthening of the suspension of disbelief, as the story in the book becomes an episode in a potentially larger narrative, something which might effectively be assimilated into man's real, foreseeable history. These effects are similar to those produced by legends, where the exotic or wonderful is ambiguously mixed with real events of a distant past and therefore assimilated into the set of events that "might have really happened after all," even if they are incredible.[3]

As Prieto-Pablos, Oziewicz, and Brawley have acknowledged, truly impactful sub-creations echo "real" myths and legends (real in the sense that they have been accepted into the canon of myths and legends), presenting and maintaining an internal plausibility that evokes a sense of "exotic" and "wonderful" possibility. And, no less importantly, these works encourage an "expansion of imagination" that simultaneously enriches one's reading experiences and gives hope for humanity's future.

This hope stems in part from the message of numinous beauty and value that Tolkien's and Herbert's mythopoeic fantasies offer readers. Such messages encourage readers to see the inherent divinity in their own environments and even in themselves. Indeed, Oziewicz explains that "fantasy is, at bottom, a holistic worldview which assumes that life is 'a continuous whole' and produces works concerned 'with the wholesomeness of the human soul or, to use a more contemporary term, the integrity of the self.'"[4] While these stories are not "real" in a conventional sense, "'there is another kind of real, one that is truer to the human spirit, demanding the pilgrim's progress to find it.'"[5] Our "creative imaginations" reveal to us "meanings," "values," and "truths that are often awesome."[6] As a result, in our participation in these stories, we enter the sub-creative process along with mythopoeic fantasists and emerge, I would hope, the better and more inspired by this literary "pilgrim's progress." Tolkien too believed that fantasy has a transcendent capacity, one that should reveal the presence of the "Divine" in our own lives: "Fantasy remains a human right: we make it in our measure and in our derivative mode, because we are made: and not only made, but made in the image and likeness of a Maker."[7] Thus, reading and writing fantasy is not simply an act of whim or fancy (though it can be entertaining and "escapist," and those too are valuable things). This genre has the potential to forge new or greater awareness of our human and our spiritual identities, and nature is, of course, a powerful way to promote this awareness. Moreover, mythopoeic fantasy can "open a door on Other Time, and if we pass through, though only for a moment, we stand outside our own time, outside Time itself, maybe."[8] The Legendarium and the Duniverse do this well; they suspend our sense of the now, allowing us fantastic escape, but they also lead us into a recoverable vision of our own world, and console us with hope for the numinous potential of that world; perhaps they even prompt us to consider action to support such potential.

For Brawley, these two potentials underlie mythopoeic fantasy's purposes. The mythopoeic fantasist not only raises awareness of the transcendent, often through depictions of nature, but he or she also points out that new consciousness to the Primary World, the reader's lived experience: "These authors are not content with simply providing readers with a renewed access to the transcendent; on the contrary, they are also attempting to create Secondary worlds to engage the reader with a new experience so that ordinary reality may be transformed through the sacramental vision."[9] This transformational quality of mythopoeic fantasy echoes that of mythology, too; among other things, mythology offers a body of knowledge and story meant to inform, delight, and inspire readers. It directs its audience to a deeper understanding and appreciation of what it means to be human, and it can also direct them to the transcendent: "Something really 'higher' is occasionally glimpsed in mythology: Divinity, the right to power (as distinct from its possession), the due of worship; in fact 'religion.'"[10] Tolkien's distinction here between the "right" to power and the "possession" of such draws parallels with both Tolkien's and Herbert's fictional worlds. As we have seen, the "heroic" characters in both imagined universes are those who follow this "higher" pattern of "divinity," who through their attitudes and actions earn their "right" to power, while the dishonorable characters demonstrate that they believe they have that right to power by merely possessing it (often through force and by underhanded means). Some of Tolkien's characters might even take hold of their rights (Frodo or Aragorn, for example) reluctantly or humbly, while others (the Atreides especially) recognize and often embrace their power as part of their lineage, but prove through action their fitness to do so. Ultimately, readers can find a transcendent, numinous experience, one that touches on the "strangeness" of fantasy, which by its very purpose needs to evoke this feeling of wonderment and strangeness. Like the effect of mythology, this experience does not need to equal a formal dogmatic religious conversion, but the goal of fantasy is not merely "escape," which (as Tolkien has so eloquently explained) in and of itself is not what readers are necessarily looking for anyway. Both the *Dune* chronicles and *The Lord of the Rings* evoke and invite this numinous experience, this "Divinity." And the treatment of nature is one of the most important ways in which these stories evoke divinity, as it is woven into the tapestry of these new mythologies.

These works further prove how important it is to continue the creation of new worlds and stories. Although they are not ancient, like other mythologies, the themes and patterns they utilize are not only timeless but also timely. Tolkien's and Herbert's love for nature and the way they frame it as sacred and worthy of respect has not lost its impact in the decades since the stories' publication, illustrating Tolkien's belief that these themes can be planted and sown again and again: "The seed of the tree can be replanted in almost any soil.... Spring is, of course, not really less beautiful because we have seen or heard of other like events: like events, never from world's beginning to world's end the same event. Each leaf, of oak and ash and thorn, is a unique embodiment of the pattern, and for some this very year may be *the* embodiment, the first ever seen and recognized, though oaks have put forth leaves for countless generations of men."[11] Mythopoeic fantasy does this, too. For some readers, it can be the embodiment of everything I and other enthusiasts think these works offer; while other stories might hold similar patterns and truths, our world needs a rich diversity of "trees"—of stories and storytellers; of the present-day concerns facing our societies and the solutions we can adopt; of the timeless convictions in hope, redemption, and compassion. Tolkien's and Herbert's works embrace these convictions and present them through their own unique visions, adding to the "the Pot of Soup, the Cauldron of Story, [which] has always been boiling, and to it have continually been added new bits, dainty and undainty."[12]

Brian Herbert shares that one of the most impactful sayings in his father's life was Ezra Pound's declaration, "Make it new."[13] His fantasy does no less than this, and Tolkien's ideas echo this mantra: "Creative fantasy, because it is mainly trying to do something else (make something new), may open your hoard and let all the locked things fly away like cage-birds. The gems all turn into flowers or flames, and you will be warned that all you had (or knew) was dangerous and potent, not really effectively chained, free and wild; no more yours than they were you."[14] Tolkien's and Herbert's mythologies take on this "potent" and "free" life, adding new variations on old themes, or new themes in familiar packaging. In their depictions of nature, especially, these writers offer more than an escape from our daily experiences; they offer "hope for [our] future,"[15] and "something, however small, to contribute to a collective healing process."[16] By resacralizing nature and creating a sense of enchantment through their storytelling, these authors are perhaps even contributing to a qualitatively *better* future, "for 'disenchanted' people will fall for the first rationalization for exploiting and destroying, and a disenchanted world doesn't feel worth defending."[17] Curry's words concur with this study's contention, that our natural spaces *are* in need of protection and defense against "exploiting and destroying." Literature is one of the ways to engage with this problem, and mythopoeic fantasy in particular offers unique perspectives and solutions. As Curry asserts, our current world is facing its own Ring: "the malevolent amalgam of the unaccountable nation-state, capitalism in the form of transnational economic power, and scientism, or the monopoly of knowledge by modern technological science"; moreover, "there are apparently no limits to its potential mastery of nature."[18] As a result, readers might be left feeling defenseless and pessimistic in the face of such uncontrollable power.

Yet, Tolkien and Herbert do not leave their readers in such a plight; their mythologies end on a note of hope, revealing some of our deepest human desires, among them "the desire of men to hold communion with other living things. . . . The magical understanding by men of the proper language of birds and beasts and trees, that is much nearer to the true purposes of Faërie."[19] While Tolkien is more specifically differentiating "beast fables" from fantasy, his comments have a resonance with what this study has asserted. Much of my argument would be purposeless if readers did not believe that "communion with other living things" and the "understanding" (magical or not) "of the proper language" of those living things was part of a holistically meaningful existence, one that encompasses the human and nonhuman worlds. Moreover, mythopoeic fantasists show readers their desire for a justice that seems at times outside of realistic possibility, a disconnect between "human" justice and that which is "legal" and "imposed by the modern state."[20] In Oziewicz's opinion, "the former fosters personal responsibility, mutual respect, and a sense of oneness with others, [but] the latter encourages facelessness, shunning personal responsibility, and frustrates our inner sense of justice."[21] Mythopoeic fantasy addresses our frustrations by its unique, near-mythological use of time, shifting from a typical "linear" path and instead stressing "repetition, phases, and eras in which nothing good is ever wasted and there is always a chance to correct wrong steps, even thousands of years later."[22] This language sounds almost ecocritical: mythopoeic fantasy does not represent a closed system of hopeless "wrong steps," doomed to be repeated; rather, it adopts modes of storytelling that reveal the human potential for true justice in our interpersonal relationships and encourages "personal responsibility, mutual respect, and a sense of oneness with others"—these ideas might have been taken directly from an ecocritical source.

Tolkien urges readers to consider the impact of mythology and fantasy, positing that works in this genre reach readers in unique ways and can indeed improve their moral character. His claims suggest that literature has a power to "preserve" mythic elements, and fantasy does so especially well: "If we pause, not merely to note that such old elements have been preserved, but to think *how* they have been preserved, we must conclude,

I think, that it has happened, often if not always, precisely because of this literary effect."[23] Tolkien's defense of the genre is validated by the popularity of his own mythopoeic fantasies, "this literary effect" bringing millions of readers to discover "such old elements" as they wander in Middle-earth. Tolkien writes that even the most unpleasant people can be molded by difficulties,[24] and that "humility and innocence—these things 'the heart of the child' must mean in such a context—do not necessarily imply an uncritical wonder, nor indeed an uncritical tenderness."[25] Consequently, the elements of mythopoeic fantasy, including the "humility and innocence" required of readers to enter "faerie"/fantasy stories, have to present "difficulties" of real consequence, ones that strike a deep chord with readers' experiences and values; the characters have to face dangers and difficult decisions, drawing the readers into this Secondary World so that they might emerge with more insight and hope for their own world. The trappings of fantasy are enjoyable, but they should serve the larger purpose of connecting with our human desires and moral awareness. As Tolkien writes, "Fantasy, the making of Other-worlds, was the heart of the desire of Faërie. I desired dragons with a profound desire. . . . But the world that contained even the imagination of Fáfnir was richer and more beautiful, at whatever cost of peril. The dweller in the quiet and fertile plains may hear of the tormented hills and the unharvested sea and long for them in his heart. For the heart is hard though the body be soft."[26] Tolkien suggests that the reward for engaging with fantasy, whether through writing or reading it (both sub-creative acts), is "richer and more beautiful" than our imaginations might at first perceive; his final line (perhaps a play on the aphorism that the flesh is weak but the spirit willing) tells readers that they have the resiliency to face fears, dangers, and unbridled desire in the worlds of mythopoeic fantasy.

Ultimately, then, we see that mythopoeic fantasy preserves many of the same patterns and themes as mythology, touching readers in emotional and psychodynamic ways that perhaps even older mythologies do not. Mythopoeic fantasy speaks to our basic fears and desires like mythology does, but it also creates characters with agency over their lives, the ability to engage with the numinous through their relationships with nature, and a pleasurable escape into their worlds that restores our own visions of our environment and ourselves. Such places as Middle-earth and Dune remain with readers for these reasons and for the inherent appeal of the places themselves. As Curry observes, Middle-earth impacts readers because of the "profound presence" of nature, which combines to create an experience of a "living and meaningful cosmos saturat[ing]" the narrative.[27] Further, he claims, "The living personality and agency of this character are none the less for being non-human; in fact, that is just what allows for a sense of ancient myth, with its feeling of a time when the Earth itself was alive. It whispers: perhaps it could be again; perhaps, indeed, it still is. And there is an accompanying sense of relief; here, at least, a reader may take refuge from a world where, as in a hall of mirrors gone mad, humanity has swollen to become everything, and the measure of everything."[28] Mythopoeic texts like those by Tolkien and Herbert restore a sense of proportion in our own world by showing us worlds that are "alive," that this is how it *should* be, and that such feelings evoked by sub-creative enchantment allow us a place of "refuge" in the face of our often confusing and overwhelming Primary World. Tolkien, too, links mythopoeic fantasy's power with words and stories to show us our real lives, albeit it in delightful and "fantastic" ways, as these stories deal actually "with simple or fundamental things, untouched by Fantasy, but these simplicities are made all the more luminous by their setting. For the story-maker who allows himself to be 'free with' Nature can be her lover not her slave."[29] These lines combine much of the effects this study has explored, including the transcendent or "numinous" qualities of the settings in mythopoeic fantasy, as well as the potential mythopoeic fantasists and readers have to engage with nature in loving, productive ways. Thus, mythopoeic fantasy does not completely rewrite our human experiences; instead, it presents them in a fresh and wondrous manner, through its "potent words" providing readers with "the wonder of the things, such as stone, and wood, and iron; tree and grass; house and fire; bread and wine."[30] Through these fantasies, our own worlds become bathed in a sacramental light, reframing stones, trees, and houses as profoundly significant pieces of these Secondary worlds and of our daily lives. As fellow mythopoeic fantasist Lloyd Alexander observes, mythopoesis is not a "'retelling or recreating [of the] ancient myth'" so much as it is "weaving 'threads from a broader mythological fabric'... with 'the personal vision that each of us has about the world he lives in.'"[31] The Legendarium and the Duniverse show us both universal values from that "broader mythological fabric" and "personal visions" of the environments we inhabit, lending a mystery and power to them that stay with us long after we turn these stories' final pages.

Paul's relationship with the desert, which so powerfully leaves readers with a sense of the myth, wonder, and interconnectedness this book has been avowing, is possible through a sacralized vision of nature. His view of Arrakis is dualistic, seeing its heat, barrenness, and potential for ugliness; yet he cannot deny its overwhelming richness, "exploding" life, and potential for beauty, and these lines of appreciation for nature are what I would like to close with: "All it required was water . . . and love. Life changed those irascible wastes into shapes of grace and movement, he thought. That was the message of the desert. Contrast stunned him with realization. He wanted to turn to the aides massed in the sietch entrance, shout at them: If you need something to worship, then worship life—all life, every last crawling bit of it! We're all in this beauty together!"[32] Readers who encounter Tolkien's Legendarium and Herbert's Duniverse can emerge from these stories with a wonderful apprehension that they, too, find the unique joy, awe, and inspiration "all life, every last crawling bit of it" has for them; that they, too, are "all in this beauty together!"

NOTES

1. MIRRORS AND THE NUMINOUS

1. Herbert, *Dreamer of Dune*, 210.
2. Here, Tolkien uses the term *fairy stories* to refer to a variety of stories that later fit under the more contemporary term *fantasy*.
3. Tolkien, "On Fairy-Stories," 114.
4. Tolkien, "On Fairy-Stories," 139.
5. Tolkien, "On Fairy-Stories," 139.
6. Tolkien, "On Fairy-Stories," 119–20.
7. See chapter 2's discussion of the "impressionistic" depictions of nature that contribute in part to such moods and atmosphere.
8. For further discussion of speculative fiction works that follow this pattern, see later chapters from Marek Oziewicz's *One Earth, One People*, Chris Brawley's *Nature and the Numinous in Mythopoeic Fantasy Literature,* and David S. Hogsett's *The Transcendent Vision of Mythopoeic Fantasy.*
9. Oziewicz, *One Earth, One People,* 84.
10. Oziewicz, *One Earth, One People,* 82.
11. Oziewicz, *One Earth, One People,* 84.
12. Tolkien, "On Fairy-Stories," 132.
13. Tolkien, "On Fairy-Stories," 139.
14. Oziewicz, *One Earth, One People,* 86.
15. Oziewicz, *One Earth, One People,* 86.
16. Oziewicz, *One Earth, One People,* 86.
17. Oziewicz, *One Earth, One People,* 87.
18. Tolkien, "On Fairy-Stories," 146.
19. See Chris Brawley's "Introduction" to *Nature and the Numinous in Mythopoeic Fantasy Literature* for a discussion of this point.

20. Another way to apprehend the power of invented beings like the Ents, and one that does not connect as overtly to the religious/sacred/numinous worldview discussed in this study, can be found in material ecocriticism (new materialism). Timothy Clark's *The Value of Ecocriticism* offers an overview of this ecocritical position and its potential to "affirm the view that non-human matter has an incalculable agency of its own" (112). In questioning anthropocentric thinking, this position also interrogates "that what are presented as basic distinctions of being—between mere passive matter and active human agency—are really political distinctions, underwriting destructive hierarchies of significance and consideration, such as 'black' as opposed to 'white,' 'female' as opposed to 'male,' and, here, a supposedly inert mere 'matter' as opposed to human 'mind' or 'spirit'" (113). Feminist ecology, or "eco-feminism," also takes up and rejects these binary, value-hierarchical modes of thinking. I offer these perspectives not to contradict the argument this study is making (that comparing Tolkien's and Herbert's mythopoeic fiction provides an essential means of understanding their ecocritical and moral positions, and that their writings sacralize nature), but rather to account for potential varieties of interpretation, particularly for readers who might find a "sacred" view of nature at odds with modern humanist values.

21. Brawley, *Nature and the Numinous*, 13.

22. As chapter 5 will show, from a young age Herbert was tied to Native American beliefs and attitudes surrounding nature as sacred, and some of his other literary works address these beliefs more overtly.

23. Herbert, *Dune*, 92.
24. Tolkien, "On Fairy-Stories," 146.
25. Le Guin, "Prophets and Mirrors," 112.
26. Le Guin, "Prophets and Mirrors," 113.
27. Le Guin, "Prophets and Mirrors," 113.
28. Tolkien, "On Fairy-Stories," 146.
29. Oziewicz, *One Earth, One People*, 82.
30. Tolkien, "On Fairy-Stories," 148.
31. Tolkien, "On Fairy-Stories," 151.
32. Tolkien, "On Fairy-Stories," 151.
33. Tolkien, "On Fairy-Stories," 153.
34. Tolkien, "On Fairy-Stories," 154.
35. Tolkien, "On Fairy-Stories," 125.
36. Curry, *Defending Middle-earth*, 17.

37. This seems to me an interesting avenue for further analysis—an extended application of Curry's ideas onto the *Dune* series would no doubt offer an expansion on the specific ways Tolkien's and Herbert's mythopoeic fiction are in conversation with each other.

38. Though some of these beings have been modified or engineered in nonhuman ways, they exhibit sentience and moral awareness in the same way the other human characters do.

39. Curry, *Defending Middle-earth*, 19.
40. Lousley, as cited in Garrard, *Ecocriticism*, 4.

41. Garrard, *Ecocriticism*, 5.
42. Oziewicz, *One Earth, One People*, 84.
43. "The strength of ecocriticism has always lain in its stress on how much the environmental crisis is one of culture and imagination." Clark, *The Value of Ecocriticism*, 159.
44. Oziewicz, *One Earth, One People*, 88.
45. Oziewicz, *One Earth, One People*, 74.
46. Clark, *Ecocriticism on the Edge*, 1.
47. Molson, as cited in Oziewicz, *One Earth, One People*, 94.
48. Tolkien, "On Fairy-Stories," 116.
49. Tolkien, "On Fairy-Stories," 143.
50. Barry Commoner's famous First Law of Ecology: "Everything is connected to everything else."
51. Tolkien, "On Fairy-Stories," 143.
52. Chapter 4 sheds light on how the language used by Tolkien and Herbert supports an ecocritical reading of their mythopoeic fantasies; chapter 5 explores possible solutions the two authors desired, drawing conclusions from their literary legacies, from what is known about their lives, and from their philosophical and political positions.
53. See Garrard, chapter 2 of *Ecocriticism* and Warren and Wells-Howe, *Ecological Feminism* for a discussion of various ecocritical positions that enumerate human-nature relationships, especially those based upon binary dualism and value-hierarchical assumptions.
54. Brawley, *Nature and the Numinous*, 15.
55. Brawley, *Nature and the Numinous*, 15.
56. In the Legendarium, for example, wizards might be regarded as quasi-religious sources of authority; Tolkien depicts their equal potential for wisdom and corruption in the form of Gandalf and Saruman, respectively; the same occurs in the Duniverse. The Bene Gesserit are the primary religious presence on Arrakis, yet Paul and his descendants frequently challenge their authority and claims to the "truth." Both depictions interrogate the integrity of such power structures.
57. Oziewicz, *One Earth, One People*, 75.
58. Tolkien, "On Fairy-Stories," 154.
59. Tolkien, "On Fairy-Stories," 156.
60. Brawley, *Nature and the Numinous*, 7–8.
61. Brawley, *Nature and the Numinous*, 9.
62. Brawley, *Nature and the Numinous*, 9.
63. Brawley, *Nature and the Numinous*, 12.
64. Cheryll Glotfelty, as cited in Brawley, *Nature and the Numinous*, 18.
65. Brawley, *Nature and the Numinous*, 18.
66. Brawley, *Nature and the Numinous*, 19.
67. Jeffers, *Arda Inhabited*.
68. Brawley, *Nature and the Numinous*, 20.
69. Brawley, *Nature and the Numinous*, 21.
70. Brawley, *Nature and the Numinous*, 22.

71. Brawley, *Nature and the Numinous*, 22. Though, as Susan Jeffers acknowledges, putting nature in a higher position than humankind merely reverses a hierarchical position of imbalanced power; later chapters on the "servanthood stewardship" model of environmental care will address the potential "benefits" of anthropocentrism.

72. Brawley, *Nature and the Numinous*, 23.

73. Brawley, *Nature and the Numinous*, 23.

74. Oziewicz, *One Earth, One People*, 81.

75. See Brian Attebery's foreword to Oziewicz, *One Earth, One People* for a discussion of these terms.

76. Oziewicz, *One Earth, One People*, 82.

77. Tolkien, "On Fairy-Stories," 134.

78. Brawley, *Nature and the Numinous*, 14.

2. FORESTS AND DESERTS

1. Garrard, *Ecocriticism*, 10.

2. Garrard, *Ecocriticism*, 7.

3. Garrard, *Ecocriticism*, 19.

4. See Garrard, *Ecocriticism*; Barry, *Beginning Theory*, 254; and Rueckert, "Literature and Ecology" among other ecocritical sources for these and other concepts significant to the study of ecocriticism.

5. Barry, *Beginning Theory*, 254.

6. See also Rueckert's discussion of literature and poems as "stored energy."

7. Clark, *The Value of Ecocriticism*, 78.

8. Clark, *The Value of Ecocriticism*, 79.

9. Barry, *Beginning Theory*, 255.

10. Curry, *Defending Middle-earth*, 17.

11. Curry, *Defending Middle-earth*, 17.

12. Dickerson and Evans and Jeffers also analyze these communities in similar terms.

13. See chapter 3 for a discussion of the Fremen and bioregionalism.

14. Herbert scholars have made the same claim of Arrakis: "As the title *Dune* already foreshadows, Arrakis's ecosystem is an active, almost sentient factor in shaping the environment and its dwellers" (Reef, "Taming Sand Dunes," 168).

15. In this sense, we can see the Shire (and other spaces within Middle-earth and the Duniverse) as operating in geocritical, as well as ecocritical, ways: "As diffuse 'schools' of criticism—the scare quotes serve to show how unreliable such a category must be in contemporary practice—ecocriticism and geocriticism represent two relatively recent and exciting discourses through which literary and cultural studies have placed renewed emphasis on the lived environment, social and natural spaces, spatiotemporality, ecology, history, and geography" (Tally and Battista, *Ecocriticism and Geocriticism*, 8). Geocriticism has as a major concern "literary representation of space and place," and questions such as "To what extent, for example, do fictional depictions of place enrich our understanding of real-world places?

More specifically, do they contribute something that other modes of representation do not?" (Prieto, "Geocriticism Meets Ecocriticism," 19, 33). A more complete geocritical interpretation of Tolkien's and Herbert's mythopoeic fantasy series would also be a needed, fruitful space for inquiry.

16. Tolkien, *Fellowship*, 5.
17. Tolkien, *Fellowship*, 6.
18. Dickerson and Evans, among other Tolkien scholars, examine the "long history" of these spaces and what significance that offers readers.
19. Jeffers, *Arda Inhabited*, 33.
20. Tolkien, *Fellowship*, 26.
21. Tolkien, *Fellowship*, 37–38.
22. Tolkien, *Fellowship*, 49.
23. Tolkien, *Fellowship*, 50.
24. Jeffers, *Arda Inhabited*, 33.
25. Herbert, *Dune*, 31.
26. Gemma Field's petrocriticism study "*Dune* Rehabilitation in Progress" examines one of the real-world engagements *Dune* prompts: "By positioning energy as integral to the matter and mechanics of human society, the text challenges the dangerous offshore discourse of oil. As the fuel of personal and political movements, the spice-melange drives the narrative and the actions of the characters, including the young duke Paul Atreides" (134), and "by highlighting the centrality of energy to modern life and culture, texts such as *Dune* frame it as an immediate and terrestrial concern" (125).
27. Herbert, *Dune*, 101.
28. Herbert, *Dune*, 101.
29. B. Herbert, *Dreamer of Dune*, 52.
30. Herbert, *Dune*, 101.
31. Herbert, *Dune*, 112.
32. Herbert, *Dune*, 244.
33. See, among other sources, Greg Garrard's review of deep ecology principles in *Ecocriticism*, 33. A primary tenant of deep ecology is the inherent worth of the nonhuman world, separate from its uses for humanity's purposes.
34. Herbert, *Dune*, 247–48.
35. Herbert, *Dune*, 248.
36. Herbert, *Dune*, 262.
37. Herbert, *Dune*, 262.
38. Akin to the passages referenced earlier describing the Shire in daytime and nighttime.
39. Herbert, *Dune*, 263.
40. Herbert, *Dune Messiah*, 47–48.
41. Herbert, *Dune Messiah*, 81.
42. See Eric Otto's *Green Speculations*, chapter 1, for an interesting exploration of the different "Arrakises" implied by the planet's prehistory—that the sandworms had transformed Arrakis before the arrival of the Harkonnens and Atreides, and that the sandworms were not necessarily native to the planet. All of this, Otto claims,

complicates and richens our understanding of the Fremen as living their "embedded" in/with nature and of "nature" not as monolithic but dynamic and shiftable.

43. See Chris Pak's chapter on terraforming in *Ecopolitical Transformations* and Nandita Biswas Mellamphy's "Terra-&-Terror Ecology" for an exploration of the complexities inherent in terraforming in the *Dune* series. "The *Dune* trilogy borrows from ecology and the pastoral to sketch a movement from terraforming seen as a positive physical and socio-cultural transformative force to terraforming as a problematic symbol of ecopolitical dictatorship and deterritorialization" (Pak, *Ecopolitical Transformations*, 124). "The terrible secret of the *Dune* chronicle is that Dune cannot be host to terra-form culture (which Herbert likens to the 'bourgeois infatuation with peaceful conservation of the past'); it can only be the medium for a culture totally submitted to the desert in which the human being is the bait for and prey of the ultimate predatory mechanism: the movement of sand, water and worm that produces the spice mélange" (Mellamphy, "Terra-&-Terror Ecology," 12).

44. Herbert, *Children of Dune*, 104.

45. Herbert, *Children of Dune*, 176.

46. Herbert, *God Emperor of Dune*, 106.

47. Herbert, *Dune*, 122.

48. Curry, *Defending Middle-earth*, 17.

49. Garrard, *Ecocriticism*, 134.

50. Garrard, *Ecocriticism*, 136.

51. Garrard, *Ecocriticism*, 143.

52. Garrard, *Ecocriticism*, 131.

53. And, I might add, hybridization fulfills Brawley's concepts of animism (nature as alive and communicative) and interrelatedness (blurring the boundary between our human and nonhuman worlds) detailed in chapter 1.

54. For a more detailed discussion of Tolkien's trees and their sentience, see Verlyn Flieger's article "Taking the Part of Trees: Eco-conflict in Middle-earth." Flieger makes an intriguing argument for the differences between various trees, Ents, and Huorns, asserting that not all of these trees *are* sentient. As I use the word, I mean a very basic definition: the ability of these trees to *feel* things. Finally, I acknowledge that Patrick Curry has said about the Ents specifically that their "glory is precisely that they are not anthropomorphic, i.e. honorary humans, but sentient trees. They share the sentience with us, and exist in relationship with us, but they are also profoundly other; and in that important sense, independent of us" (Curry, *Deep Roots*, 50–51). I do not disagree with Curry, though within the typological framework provided by Garrard, I see both the Ents and Tolkien's other "trees" as akin to anthropomorphism in how they encourage readers to identify a positive, ecoconscious likeness. However, I can recognize the value in the Ents' potential allomorphic "otherness" too.

55. Tolkien, *Fellowship*, 125.

56. See Dickerson and Evans, *Ents, Elves, and Eriador*, 137, for more analysis of these passages and the Old Forest generally.

57. Tolkien, *Fellowship*, 125.

58. Indeed, Flieger's analysis of this "menace" reveals, in her opinion, contradictions in Tolkien's portrayal of trees—he claims to always take the side of trees,

yet his characterizations are at times problematic. While I do not fully agree with Flieger's analysis, it leaves open an interesting dialogue about Tolkien's trees. Liam Campbell's afterword "Trouble with the Trees" in *The Ecological Augury* picks up this discussion and is another useful study to examine Tolkien's depiction of trees.

59. Tolkien, *Fellowship*, 125.

60. Tolkien, *Fellowship*, 126.

61. Dickerson and Evans frame the significance of spaces like the Old Forest as follows: "people are not always friendly toward the environment—toward wilderness in particular—and, in response, the environment is not always friendly toward people. In Middle-earth, as in our world, mistreatment of the natural world results in an environment that is less hospitable to its inhabitants" and "disharmony . . . is only the secondary response of an endangered environment" (*Ents, Elves, and Eriador*, 140).

62. Flieger, "The Forest and the Trees," 156.

63. Chapter 3 explores Fanghorn as a complex space; as I've limited my study to the main trilogy, I am not presenting a detailed discussion of Mirkwood, though other scholars such as Dickerson and Evans and Flieger address that forest in enlightening ways.

64. I want to be careful here not to imply that humans should just give up and let forests take over everywhere; instead, to be thoughtful of whether our needs are legitimate or only for our own convenience. If the latter, it's a slippery slope from convenience to unnecessary destruction. The principles of Deep Ecology are in conversation with this idea of balancing necessary human needs with the richness and diversity of nonhuman life.

65. Tolkien, *Fellowship*, 130.

66. See Dickerson and Evans, *Ents, Elves, and Eriador*; Campbell, *The Ecological Augury*; and Flieger, "Taking the Part of Trees" for more discussion of Old Man Willow.

67. Herbert, *Dune*, 242.

68. The Fremen are all spice-dependent; without the sandworms, there would be no spice, and thus Fremen existence would be drastically altered. "The sandworm life cycle and desert world-building served to elucidate ecological interdependence and the risks of interference with nature in a subtle parable" (Reef, "Taming Sand Dunes," 166).

69. Herbert, *Dune*, 512.

70. Keep in mind the "mythic association" as opposed to "mythic disassociation" referenced in chapter 1—that the divine is present and accessible in the natural world, not necessarily in or only in the transcendent.

71. The "interrelatedness" in ecocritical mythopoeic fiction Brawley has written about.

72. Tolkien, *Fellowship*, 253.

73. Dickerson and Evans analyze this "otherworldly . . . perfection," likening it to Valinor (*Ents, Elves, and Eriador*, 106).

74. Tolkien, *Fellowship*, 268.

75. Brawley, *Nature and the Numinous*, 110.

76. Brawley, *Nature and the Numinous*, 110.

77. "Elves . . . appreciate the inherent beauty of the things they have worked to

preserve as a group over time," and Legolas intends to "share" the joy he finds from appreciating the beauties of nature (Jeffers, *Arda Inhabited*, 43).

78. Tolkien, *Fellowship*, 375.

79. In the Legendarium, colors take on important meaning, which Flieger and others have also analyzed.

80. Jeffers, *Arda Inhabited*, 61.

81. Brawley, *Nature and the Numinous*, 109.

82. Brawley, *Nature and the Numinous*, 109.

83. Brawley, *Nature and the Numinous*, 109.

84. Tolkien, *Fellowship*, 405.

85. Brawley, *Nature and the Numinous*, 109.

86. Brawley, *Nature and the Numinous*, 109–10.

87. Tolkien, *Fellowship*, 391.

88. Herbert, *Chapterhouse: Dune*, 13–14.

89. Herbert, *Chapterhouse: Dune*, 13.

90. Edward John Royston's "*Dune* and the Metanarrative of Power" examines the Bene Gesserit's control of texts and stories as yet another way they exert power.

91. Tolkien, *The Two Towers*, 15.

92. Tolkien, *The Two Towers*, 127.

93. See chapter 2 of *Arda Inhabited* for Jeffers's analysis of Rohan, Gondor, and other human communities as spaces of the "power from" environmental model.

94. Tolkien, *Return of the King*, 8.

95. Tolkien, *Return of the King*, 152.

96. In these passages, Tolkien is blending "real" environmental harm caused by Saruman's industrialization, but also "perceived" harm (as this company does not yet realize how the Ents have flooded Isengard to remove Saruman's destructive presence and begin cleansing the land).

97. Tolkien, *The Two Towers*, 169.

98. Tolkien, *The Two Towers*, 173. Dickerson and Evans analyze this and other passages in light of the harmful environmental model embodied by Saruman and Sauron.

99. Tolkien, *The Two Towers*, 173.

100. Tolkien, *The Two Towers*, 174.

101. Tolkien, *The Two Towers*, 259.

102. Jeffers frames the choices of Saruman and Sauron as the "power over" environmental model, that of oppression.

103. Tolkien, *Return of the King*, 184.

104. Tolkien, *Return of the King*, 210.

105. Tolkien, *Return of the King*, 212.

106. Dickerson and Evans, *Ents, Elves, and Eriador*, 186.

107. Herbert, *Heretics of Dune*, 387.

108. Herbert, *Chapterhouse: Dune*, 33.

109. Tolkien, *Return of the King*, 211.

110. Mythopoeic fantasy's "consolation" of hope as a radical force in the face of real and significant moral corruption.

3. HALFLINGS AND HARKONNENS

1. Howarth, "Some Principles of Ecocriticism," 69.
2. Jeffers, *Arda Inhabited*, 51.
3. Jeffers, *Arda Inhabited*, 17.
4. Jeffers, *Arda Inhabited*, 17–18. Liam Campbell observes that "Middle-earth may be best described as a character that is slowly dying, dying at the hands of other characters who attack it relentlessly—both willfully and as a consequence of other goals, but always without justifiable cause" (*The Ecological Augury*, 180). Arrakis/Dune's eventual death echoes this description.
5. Jeffers, *Arda Inhabited*, 4.
6. Tolkien, *Fellowship*, 1–2.
7. Dickerson and Evans, *Ents, Elves, and Eriador*, 84.
8. Jeffers, *Arda Inhabited*, 33.
9. Jeffers, *Arda Inhabited*, 33.
10. Jeffers, *Arda Inhabited*, 35.
11. Curry, *Defending Middle-earth*, 28.
12. See Greg Garrard's chapter 3: "Pastoral" in *Ecocriticism* for a discussion of the pastoral as an ecocritical concept, including critiques and misunderstandings of the concept.
13. Dickerson and Evans, *Ents, Elves, and Eriador*, 73.
14. Dickerson and Evans, *Ents, Elves, and Eriador*, 73.
15. Dickerson and Evans, *Ents, Elves, and Eriador*, 74.
16. Curry, *Defending Middle-earth*, 29.
17. Tolkien, *Fellowship*, 35.
18. Tolkien, *Fellowship*, 35.
19. Curry, *Defending Middle-earth*, 33.
20. Tolkien, *Fellowship*, 91.
21. Tolkien, *Fellowship*, 93.
22. Tolkien, *Fellowship*, 93.
23. Dickerson and Evans, *Ents, Elves, and Eriador*, 83, 91.
24. Dickerson and Evans, *Ents, Elves, and Eriador*, 75.
25. Jeffers, *Arda Inhabited*, 38.
26. Herbert, *Dune*, 3.
27. Jeffers details the notion of "dwelling" (having been in a place for a length of time in order to know it and thus have "power with" nature); in this sense, Paul is different from the Hobbits.
28. O'Reilly, *Frank Herbert*, 50.
29. Herbert, *Dune*, 27.
30. Howarth, "Some Principles of Ecocriticism," 69.
31. Herbert, *Dune*, 373.
32. See Jeffers's discussion of Tom Bombadil in *Arda Inhabited*: "[He] is perhaps the ultimate example of this kind of connectivity that validates others without undermining one's sense of self. He is completely at home in his place. He speaks to it and understands it. He is able to influence it for the better without attempting to

dominate it" (25). See also Liam Campbell's consideration of the character in *The Ecological Augury* as akin to the legend of the Green Man: "Perhaps more than any other characteristic, however, it is Tom Bombadil's 'vow of poverty,' his renunciation of power and his desire not to exploit but to live in harmony with the world around him that most aligns him with the legend of the Green Man" (94). Chapter 1 in Dickerson and Evans's *Ents, Elves, and Eriador* analyzes Tom Bombadil's eco-consciousness as well.

33. Tolkien, *Fellowship*, 140–41.
34. Dickerson and Evans, *Ents, Elves, and Eriador*, 22.
35. Campbell, *The Ecological Augury*, 95.
36. Campbell, *The Ecological Augury*, 105.
37. Tolkien, *Fellowship*, 137.
38. Tolkien, *Fellowship*, 136.
39. Tolkien, *Fellowship*, 137.
40. Campbell, *The Ecological Augury*, 76–77. He writes that "Just in attending to Tom's words the hobbits begin to take account of other living things, to develop, one might say, their environmental conscience. Yet Tom offers no idealized portrayal of nature—the 'evil,' 'unfriendly' and 'cruel things' he sings of do not exclusively refer to dark lords or orcs, but also to the harsh reality of nature as it is."
41. Tolkien, *The Two Towers*, 64.
42. Tolkien, *The Two Towers*, 75.
43. Tolkien, *The Two Towers*, 75.
44. Daniel Gustav Anderson interrogates the Fremen and power as part of a critical bioregionalist framework:

> The cultural experience of the Fremen of Arrakis represents both these claims in that the Fremen as members of a fractured proletariat are wholly marginalized by and vulnerable to the capricious whims of a sovereign power. In other words, they occupy a position where power meets bare life; they are the "many-headed hydra" against which the Hercules of capital has been pitted from the start . . . But this multitude also has the potential to become a disciplined force, sweeping off the sea of the desert into the polis from the edges . . . A democratization of land and labor is an alternative to the jihad Muad'Dib most fears. . . . The Fremen have become uniquely creative and capable by virtue of their bioregional experience, but not fulfilled or self-directed due to their position and manipulation by powers beyond their control: the Imperium, Paul and his mother, the Guild, the Bene Gesserit. This lack of direction can be ameliorated by a coherent and properly implemented program for bioregional control. ("Critical Bioregionalist Method," 236)

45. Anderson, "Critical Bioregionalist Method," 236.
46. Herbert, *Dune*, 211.
47. Herbert, *Dune*, 281.
48. See again Eric Otto's analysis of the Fremen as "embedded" with nature, employing Deep Ecology values, in his first chapter of *Green Speculations*.
49. Herbert, *Dune*, 310.
50. Herbert, *Dune*, 310.

51. Herbert, *Dune,* 310.
52. Herbert, *Dune,* 311.
53. However, Peter Herman sees Liet-Kynes as the truer Christ-figure:

> Liet-Kynes dies to the whiteness of empire and exploitation before we meet him. Recall that he is both the Imperial Planetologist and the Judge of the Change, charged with ensuring that the transfer of power from Harkonnen to Atreides is lawful and appropriate. It is from this position that he acts in subversion of the aims of empire. Should Arrakis become an arable climate, the great sandworms that supply the necessary spice will become extinct. His plan is to slowly and gradually create a paradise for the Fremen. This must necessarily come at the expense of the empire. His actions, then are not the simple inversion of Paul/Muad'Dib, but rather a subversion and—indeed—a transvaluation of values. Like Christ, he dies humiliated and alone, calling out to a father who may not hear him. Yet Herbert puts him in the analogous role of John the Baptist, proclaiming the coming messiah. For Herbert's novel, the messiah who comes does not bring subversion, liberation, or transvaluation. He brings only a different emperor for the same empire. ("The Blackness of Liet-Kynes," 10)

(Interestingly, Denis Villeneuve's 2021 film adaptation, *Dune,* figures Kynes literally as a Black female character. While Herman is writing of Blackness as not just literal but rather a theological position via James Cone, our understanding of Kynes shifts when figuring him or her as "not-white.")

54. Herbert, *Dune,* 264.
55. Herbert, *Dune,* 264.
56. Herbert, *Dune,* 265.
57. Herbert, *Dune,* 265.
58. Herbert, *Dune,* 265.
59. Herbert, 265.
60. Herbert, *Dune,* 265.
61. B. Herbert, *Dreamer of Dune,* 181.
62. Though, in later novels, a few Bene Gesserit break this mold, finding more direct and valuable relationships with other people and environments.
63. Herbert, *Dune,* 3.
64. Herbert, *Dune,* 6.
65. See chapters 4 and 5 for a review of Paul and Jessica's embrace of the Fremen community and what significance we can derive from that.
66. Herbert, *Dune,* 48.
67. Though, true to the theme of ambivalence throughout the Duniverse, Paul does indeed become immersed in both past and present after his "awakening."
68. Herbert, *Dune,* 381.
69. Herbert, *Dune,* 277.
70. Herbert, *Dune,* 280.
71. Herbert, *Dune,* 311.
72. Herbert, *Dune,* 285.

73. See Dickerson and Evans, *Ents, Elves, and Eriador,* 230, and chapter 2 of Jeffers, *Arda Inhabited* for more ecocritical analysis of Gimli and Dwarves.
74. Tolkien, *The Two Towers,* 354.
75. Jeffers frames them as "interrelated" to their environment.
76. Tolkien, *The Two Towers,* 145.
77. Tolkien, *The Two Towers,* 231.
78. Dickerson and Evans analyze Mordor in their chapter "Three Faces of Mordor":

> The evils of Sauron and the dangers he poses to the ecology of Middle-earth are threefold: they appear in descriptions of the land of Mordor itself, in portrayals of Saruman's Isengard, and in the picture of a degraded Shire under Sharkey at the end of the story. Such a presentation not only enables readers to see the natural (or, rather, *anti*-natural) conclusion of Sauron's ecological nightmare but also provides—in images of the Shire under hostile occupation—a more realistic and accessible picture that comes much closer to home. Readers are shown what Mordor looks like when it is no longer far away but has come into their own backyards. (*Ents, Elves, and Eriador,* 185)

79. Tolkien, *Return of the King,* 266.
80. Herbert, *Dune,* 226.
81. Herbert, *Dune,* 232.
82. Herbert, *Dune,* 232–33.
83. Herbert, *Dune,* 233–34.
84. Herbert, *Dune,* 234.
85. Herbert, *Dune,* 318.
86. Herbert, *Dune,* 445.
87. Herbert, *Dune,* 472.
88. Tolkien, *Fellowship,* 299.
89. Campbell examines Gandalf's environmental ethics in chapter 3 of *The Ecological Augury.*
90. See chapter 4's discussion of Sam too.
91. Tolkien, *The Two Towers,* 11.
92. Tolkien, *The Two Towers,* 28.
93. Tolkien, *The Two Towers,* 29.

4. NATURE'S VOICE

1. Oziewicz, *One Earth, One People,* 89.
2. Oziewicz, *One Earth, One People,* 89.
3. Oziewicz, *One Earth, One People,* 89.
4. Mendlesohn, *Rhetorics of Fantasy,* 32.
5. Mendlesohn, *Rhetorics of Fantasy,* 33.
6. Mendlesohn, *Rhetorics of Fantasy,* 34.
7. Shippey, *The Road to Middle-earth,* 66–67.

8. Day, *The Hobbit Companion*, 11.
9. Day, *The Hobbit Companion*, 11–13.
10. Flieger, *Splintered Light*, 148–49.
11. Jeffers, *Arda Inhabited*, 33.
12. Day, *The Hobbit Companion*, 19.
13. Noel, *The Languages of Tolkien's Middle-earth*, 33.
14. Noel, *The Languages of Tolkien's Middle-earth*, 33.
15. Flieger, *Splintered Light*, 7.
16. "Gollum is a wanderer, and his complex, unique 'power with' relationship with the land of Mordor is emblematic of his broken inability to find true community anywhere" (Jeffers, *Arda Inhabited*, 94–95).
17. Flieger, *Splintered Light*, 7.
18. Grotta, *Architect of Middle-earth*, 96.
19. Shippey, *J. R. R. Tolkien*, 14–17.
20. Day, *The Hobbit Companion*, 52.
21. Day, *The Hobbit Companion*, 52.
22. Noel, *The Languages of Tolkien's Middle-earth*, 32.
23. Day, *The Hobbit Companion*, 52.
24. Interestingly, Ilúvatar's own name conveys a sense of his nature as well, deriving from words meaning *the whole, the all, universe,* and elsewhere *the One*. "Name and epithet are thus conceptually, though not etymologically or phonologically, related. The shift from 'one' to 'whole' to 'all' is itself indicative of a change in perception and/or consciousness from an indivisible unity to a whole (as opposed to part) to a totality or collection" (Flieger, *Splintered Light*, 50).
25. Jeffers, *Arda Inhabited*, 106.
26. For a more complete discussion of Gandalf's model of stewardship, see chapter 2 of Dickerson and Evans, *Ents, Elves, and Eriador*.
27. Shippey, *J. R. R. Tolkien*, 169; Day, *The Hobbit Companion*, 52.
28. Noel, *The Languages of Tolkien's Middle-earth*, 28.
29. Noel, *The Languages of Tolkien's Middle-earth*, 27.
30. Day, *The Hobbit Companion*, 52.
31. Dickerson and Evans, Jeffers, Flieger, and Campbell have all examined similar aspects of Saruman's disconnected nature.
32. Jeffers, *Arda Inhabited*, 89.
33. Flieger, *Splintered Light*, 158.
34. Flieger, *Splintered Light*, 159.
35. Noel, *The Languages of Tolkien's Middle-earth*, 189.
36. Day, *The Hobbit Companion*, 82.
37. Jeffers, *Arda Inhabited*, 93.
38. Jeffers, *Arda Inhabited*, 93.
39. Flieger, *Splintered Light*, 150.
40. And Campbell positions Sauron as the opposite model of environmental relations to Gandalf.
41. Noel, *The Languages of Tolkien's Middle-earth*; Day, *The Hobbit Companion*.

42. Noel, *The Languages of Tolkien's Middle-earth,* 172.
43. Jeffers, *Arda Inhabited,* 87. See also Hood's "Sauron and Dracula."
44. Tyler, *The Tolkien Companion,* 309.
45. Flieger, *Splintered Light,* 74.
46. Flieger, *Splintered Light,* 75.
47. Flieger, *Splintered Light,* 75.
48. Flieger, *Splintered Light,* 75.
49. Jeffers, *Arda Inhabited,* 55.
50. Flieger, *Splintered Light,* 75.
51. Noel, *The Languages of Tolkien's Middle-earth,* 20.
52. Shippey, *J. R. R. Tolkien,* 184.
53. Day, *The Hobbit Companion,* 83. See also Shippey, *J. R. R. Tolkien,* 185–86.
54. Day, *The Hobbit Companion,* 83.
55. Shippey is quick to point out that Frodo is not an allegorical Christ figure but "something related" (*J. R. R. Tolkien,* 187).
56. Jeffers, *Arda Inhabited,* 108.
57. Jeffers, *Arda Inhabited,* 108.
58. Dickerson and Evans, *Ents, Elves, and Eriador,* 18, 155.
59. B. Herbert, *Dreamer of Dune,* 169.
60. B. Herbert, *Dreamer of Dune,* 72.
61. B. Herbert, *Dreamer of Dune,* 180.
62. Kennedy, "Epic World-Building," 110.
63. Kennedy, "Epic World-Building," 100.
64. Kennedy, "Epic World-Building," 100.
65. Kennedy, "Epic World-Building," 101.
66. Kennedy, "Epic World-Building," 101.
67. Kennedy, "Epic World-Building," 101–2.
68. Kennedy, "Epic World-Building," 101.
69. Kennedy, "Epic World-Building," 105.
70. Kennedy also details the relevance of Paul's other names, such as Usul and Lisan al-Gaib.
71. See Palumbo's "The Monomyth as Fractal Pattern," "The Monomyth and Chaos Theory," and "'Plots within Plots.'"
72. Parkerson, "Semantics," 410.
73. There are numerous examples of ecological semantics in the five sequels; however, for purposes of length and focus, this chapter will use *Dune* as a case study, asserting that the patterns Herbert has used in *Dune* emerge in the sequels, too.
74. Touponce, *Frank Herbert,* 13–14.
75. Touponce, *Frank Herbert,* 2.
76. O'Reilly, *Frank Herbert,* 13.
77. Abrams, *A Glossary of Literary Terms,* 267.
78. Abrams, *A Glossary of Literary Terms,* 267.
79. O'Reilly, *Frank Herbert,* 55.
80. Herbert, *The Maker of Dune,* 100.

81. Stephenson, *Snow Crash*, 394–95.

82. In Middle-earth, too, words create and hold power; one example that comes to mind is Black Speech, the language of Sauron, inscribed on the One Ring and which Gandalf is reluctant to speak aloud.

83. Herbert, *Dune*, 30.

84. Herbert, *The Maker of Dune*, 100.

85. Herbert, *Dune*, 30.

86. I discussed this same passage in chapter 2, though for purposes of demonstrating the numinous qualities that Herbert's language evokes. To be clear, here I am using the passage to support a separate claim.

87. Herbert, *Dune*, 263.

88. Herbert, *Dune*, 262–63.

89. Herbert, *The Maker of Dune*, 99.

90. Touponce, *Frank Herbert*, 12.

91. Deutscher, *Through the Language Glass*, 188–91.

92. Deutscher, *Through the Language Glass*, 192.

93. In later novels, other characters, especially Leto II, can also use it to great effect and for significant purposes, particularly in defense of Dune and its resources. While not analyzing Leto's "Voice" specifically, Michael Phillips has observed that Leto engages in a "dialectical" (interestingly, Jeffers uses this as a way to understand the "power from" model of environmental relations), understanding existence not as a "struggle" based on "annihilat[ion]. Rather, a dialectic emerges through which conflict does not resolve in some final, triumphant outcome but instead is a continual process in which organisms improve themselves and their chances for survival. Leto extends this ecological viewpoint to his political philosophy" (Reef, "Taming Sand Dunes," 47).

94. Oziewicz, *One Earth, One People*, 90.

95. Another obvious parallel to the Voice in Tolkien's writing would be, among other examples, Saruman's voice. See *The Two Towers* chapter, "The Voice of Saruman," as well as Shippey's treatment of Saruman's voice beginning on page 126 in *J. R. R. Tolkien: Author of the Century*. Shippey sees Saruman's corruption as "wraithlike," "partly by merging himself with his own cause, discarding any sense of means in pursuit of some increasingly impossible end, and partly by the self-deceptions of language" (126). In this sense, then, while Saruman's voice exerts power in a similar manner to Paul's and Jessica's Voices, it is dissimilar in its eventual betrayal and "self-deception" of the wielder, Saruman.

96. B. Herbert, *Dreamer of Dune*, 177.

97. Herbert, *Dune*, 135.

98. Herbert, *Dune*, 134–35.

99. Herbert, *Dune*, 166.

100. Herbert, *Dune*, 192.

101. Herbert, *Dune*, 333.

102. Herbert, *Dune*, 413–14.

103. Herbert, *Dune*, 419–20.

104. B. Herbert, *Dreamer of Dune*, 177–78. See also Royston, "*Dune* and the Metanarratives of Power."
105. Herbert, *Dune*, 462–63.
106. Of course, there has been necessary and fruitful debate about whether Paul's leadership is indeed ethical. Within the context of the above passage, Paul stands, at least for a moment, as a proponent of "righteousness."
107. Herbert, *Dune*, 108.
108. Herbert, *Dune*, 303.
109. Herbert, *Dune*, 237.
110. Touponce, *Frank Herbert*, 21.
111. Touponce, *Frank Herbert*, 21.
112. Touponce, *Frank Herbert*, 23.
113. Herbert, *Dune*, 133–34.
114. Herbert, *Dune*, 5.
115. O'Reilly, *Frank Herbert*, 59–60.
116. Touponce, *Frank Herbert*, 3.
117. Touponce, *Frank Herbert*, 3.
118. Touponce, *Frank Herbert*, 8–9.
119. Touponce, *Frank Herbert*, 16.
120. Touponce, *Frank Herbert*, 14.
121. Touponce, *Frank Herbert*, 16.
122. Touponce, *Frank Herbert*, 19.
123. Touponce, *Frank Herbert*, 20.
124. A more complete exploration of quasi-direct discourse within Tolkien's mythopoeic fantasy would, of course, be welcome. In lieu of that, I recommend Shippey and Flieger (among many other Tolkien scholars) as sources for deep and insightful linguistic analyses.
125. Touponce, *Frank Herbert*, 20–21.
126. Oziewicz, *One Earth, One People*, 90.

5. "TO HOLD COMMUNION WITH LIVING THINGS"

1. Carpenter, *J. R. R. Tolkien*, 9.
2. Carpenter, *J. R. R. Tolkien*, 9.
3. Carpenter, *J. R. R. Tolkien*, 28–29.
4. Grotta, *Architect of Middle-earth*, 22.
5. Grotta, *Architect of Middle-earth*, 21.
6. Carpenter, *J. R. R. Tolkien*, 30.
7. Grotta, *Architect of Middle-earth*, 21–22.
8. Grotta, *Architect of Middle-earth*, 21.
9. B. Herbert, *Dreamer of Dune*, 25.
10. B. Herbert, *Dreamer of Dune*, 25.
11. Birzer, as cited in Jeffers, *Arda Inhabited*, 37.

12. Ball, as cited in Jeffers, *Arda Inhabited*, 37.
13. Jeffers, *Arda Inhabited*, 38.
14. Dickerson and Evans, *Ents, Elves, and Eriador*, 88.
15. Tolkien, *Return of the King*, 268.
16. Tolkien, *Return of the King*, 269.
17. Tolkien, *Return of the King*, 277.
18. Tolkien, *Return of the King*, 322.
19. Dickerson and Evans, too, point to the emotional effect of this scene.
20. Tolkien, *Return of the King*, 331.
21. Tolkien, *Return of the King*, 338.
22. Tolkien, *Return of the King*, 160.
23. Tolkien, *Return of the King*, 162.
24. Tolkien, *Return of the King*, 131.
25. Tolkien, *Return of the King*, 131.
26. Dickerson and Evans, *Ents, Elves, and Eriador*, 37.
27. B. Herbert, *Dreamer of Dune*, 102.
28. Jeffers, *Arda Inhabited*, 122.
29. Grotta, *Architect of Middle-earth*, 25.
30. B. Herbert, *Dreamer of Dune*, 147.
31. B. Herbert, *Dreamer of Dune*, 96.
32. B. Herbert, *Dreamer of Dune*, 123.
33. Carpenter, *J. R. R. Tolkien*, 39.
34. Dickerson and Evans, *Ents, Elves, and Eriador*, 89.
35. B. Herbert, *Dreamer of Dune*, 21.
36. B. Herbert, *Dreamer of Dune*, 21.
37. B. Herbert, *Dreamer of Dune*, 190.
38. B, Herbert, *Dreamer of Dune*, 190.
39. B. Herbert, *Dreamer of Dune*, 21.
40. B. Herbert, *Dreamer of Dune*, 33.
41. B. Herbert, *Dreamer of Dune*, 33.
42. B. Herbert, *Dreamer of Dune*, 431.
43. B. Herbert, *Dreamer of Dune*, 190.
44. B. Herbert, *Dreamer of Dune*, 142.
45. Stratton, "Messiah and the Greens," 307.
46. Stratton, "Messiah and the Greens," 307.
47. B. Herbert, *Dreamer of Dune*, 155.
48. B. Herbert, *Dreamer of Dune*, 155.
49. B. Herbert, *Dreamer of Dune*, 155.
50. Herbert, *Dune Messiah*, 135.
51. Herbert, *Dune Messiah*, 271.
52. Herbert, *Children of Dune*, 280.
53. Herbert, *Children of Dune*, 280.
54. Prieto-Pablos, "The Ambivalent Hero," 72.
55. Jeffers, *Arda Inhabited*, 32.
56. Prieto-Pablos, "The Ambivalent Hero," 73.

57. B. Herbert, *Dreamer of Dune,* 72.
58. Herbert, *Children of Dune,* 175.
59. B. Herbert, *Dreamer of Dune,* 157.
60. Curry, *Defending Middle-earth,* 37.
61. Otto, *Green Speculations,* 35.
62. B. Herbert, *Dreamer of Dune,* 27.
63. Herbert, *Children of Dune,* 89.
64. Herbert, *Children of Dune,* 209.
65. Detailed comparisons of these various works (some of which certainly have been published) would no doubt be valuable; for purposes of brevity, I am making more general comparisons. Nevertheless, I do not want to do a disservice to the complexity and profundity of these authors' works.
66. B. Herbert, *Dreamer of Dune,* 185.
67. Tolkien, *Letters,* 289.

CONCLUSION

1. Abrams, *A Glossary of Literary Terms,* 53.
2. Abrams, *A Glossary of Literary Terms,* 53.
3. Prieto-Pablos, "The Ambivalent Hero," 67.
4. Egoff, as cited in Oziewicz, *One Earth, One People,* 68.
5. Oziewicz, *One Earth, One People,* 68.
6. Oziewicz, *One Earth, One People,* 68.
7. Tolkien, "On Fairy-Stories," 145.
8. Tolkien, "On Fairy-Stories," 128–29.
9. Brawley, *Nature and the Numinous,* 17.
10. Tolkien, "On Fairy-Stories," 124.
11. Tolkien, "On Fairy-Stories," 145.
12. Tolkien, "On Fairy-Stories," 125.
13. B. Herbert, *Dreamer of Dune,* 35.
14. Tolkien, "On Fairy-Stories," 147.
15. Curry, *Defending Middle-earth,* 23.
16. Curry, *Defending Middle-earth,* 19.
17. Curry, *Defending Middle-earth,* 59.
18. Curry, *Defending Middle-earth,* 67.
19. Tolkien, "On Fairy-Stories," 117.
20. Oziewicz, *One Earth, One People,* 89.
21. Oziewicz, *One Earth, One People,* 89.
22. Oziewicz, *One Earth, One People,* 89.
23. Tolkien, "On Fairy-Stories," 129.
24. Tolkien, "On Fairy-Stories," 136.
25. Tolkien, "On Fairy-Stories," 136.
26. Tolkien, "On Fairy-Stories," 135.
27. Curry, *Defending Middle-earth,* 50.

28. Curry, *Defending Middle-earth*, 50.
29. Tolkien, "On Fairy-Stories," 147.
30. Tolkien, "On Fairy-Stories," 147.
31. As cited in Oziewicz, *One Earth, One People*, 153.
32. Herbert, *Dune Messiah*, 300–301.

BIBLIOGRAPHY

Abrams, M. H. *A Glossary of Literary Terms*. 9th ed. Boston: Wadsworth, 2009.
Anderson, Daniel Gustav. "Critical Bioregionalist Method in *Dune:* A Position Paper." In *The Bioregional Imagination: Literature, Ecology, and Place*, 226–42. Athens: Univ. of Georgia Press, 2012.
Baratta, Chris. *Environmentalism in the Realm of Science Fiction and Fantasy Literature*. Cambridge: Cambridge Scholars, 2012.
Barry, Peter. *Beginning Theory: An Introduction to Literary and Cultural Theory*. 3rd ed. Manchester: Manchester Univ. Press, 2009.
Brawley, Chris. *Nature and the Numinous in Mythopoeic Fantasy Literature*. Jefferson, NC: McFarland, 2014.
Campbell, Liam. *The Ecological Augury in the Works of J. R. R. Tolkien*. Zurich and Jena: Walking Tree Publishers, 2011.
Carpenter, Humphrey. *J. R. R. Tolkien: A Biography*. Boston: Houghton Mifflin, 2000.
Clark, Timothy. *Ecocriticism on the Edge*. London: Bloomsbury, 2015.
———. *The Value of Ecocriticism*. Cambridge: Cambridge Univ. Press, 2019.
Curry, Patrick. *Deep Roots in a Time of Frost: Essays on Tolkien*. Zurich and Jena: Walking Tree Publishers, 2014.
———. *Defending Middle-earth*. Boston: Houghton Mifflin, 2004.
Day, David. *The Hobbit Companion*. New York: Metro, 1997.
Deutscher, Guy. *Through the Language Glass*. London: Picador, 2011.
Dickerson, Matthew T., and Jonathan Evans. *Ents, Elves, and Eriador: The Environmental Vision of J. R. R. Tolkien*. Lexington: Univ. Press of Kentucky, 2011.
Edwards, Raymond. *Tolkien*. London: Robert Hale, 2014.
Elgin, Don D. *The Comedy of the Fantastic: Ecological Perspectives on the Fantasy Novel*. Westport, CT: Greenwood, 1985.

Field, Gemma. "*Dune* Rehabilitation in Progress." *Journal of Literary Studies* 34, no. 3 (2018): 123–37.

Flieger, Verlyn. "The Forest and the Trees: Sal and Ian in Faërie." *There Would Always Be a Fairy Tale: More Essays on Tolkien.* Kent, OH: Kent State Univ. Press, 2017.

———. *Splintered Light: Logos and Language in Tolkien's World.* Rev. ed. Kent, OH: Kent State Univ. Press, 2002.

———. "Taking the Part of Trees: Eco-conflict in Middle-earth." *Green Suns and Faërie.* Kent, OH: Kent State Univ. Press, 2012.

———. "Words and World-Making: The Particle Physics of Middle-earth." *There Would Always Be a Fairy Tale: More Essays on Tolkien.* Kent, OH: Kent State Univ. Press, 2017.

Garrard, Greg. *Ecocriticism.* 3rd ed. London: Routledge, 2023.

Glotfelty, Cheryll. "Introduction: Literary Studies in an Age of Environmental Crisis." In *The Ecocriticism Reader,* edited by Cheryll Glotfelty and Harold Fromm, xv–xxxvii. Athens: Univ. of Georgia Press, 1996.

Grotta, Daniel. *J. R. R. Tolkien: Architect of Middle Earth.* Philadelphia: Running Press, 1992.

Herbert, Brian. *Dreamer of Dune: The Biography of Frank Herbert.* New York: Tor, 2003.

Herbert, Frank. *Chapterhouse: Dune.* New York: Ace, 1985.

———. *Children of Dune.* New York: Ace, 1976.

———. *Dune.* New York: Ace, 1965.

———. *Dune Messiah.* New York: Ace, 1969.

———. *God Emperor of Dune.* New York: Ace, 1981.

———. *Heretics of Dune.* New York: Ace, 1984.

———. *The Maker of Dune.* Edited by Tim O'Reilly. New York: Berkley Books, 1987.

Herman, Peter. "The Blackness of Liet-Kynes: Reading Frank Herbert's *Dune* through James Cone." *Religions* 9, no. 9 (2018): 281.

Hilton, James. *Lost Horizon.* New York: Pocket Books, 1973.

Hogsette, David S. *The Transcendent Vision of Mythopoeic Fantasy.* Jefferson, NC: McFarland, 2022.

Hood, Gwyneth. "Sauron and Dracula." *Mythlore* 14, no. 2 (Winter 1987): 11–17.

Howarth, William. "Some Principles of Ecocriticism." In *The Ecocriticism Reader,* edited by Cheryll Glotfelty and Harold Fromm, 69–91. Athens: Univ. of Georgia Press, 1996.

Jeffers, Susan. *Arda Inhabited: Environmental Relationships in* The Lord of the Rings. Kent, OH: Kent State Univ. Press, 2014.

Kennedy, Kara. "Epic World-Building: Names and Cultures in *Dune.*" *Names* 64, no. 2 (2016): 99–108.

———. "The Softer Side of *Dune:* The Impact of the Social Sciences on World-Building." In *Exploring Imaginary Worlds: Essays on Media, Structure, and Subcreation,* edited by J. P. Wolf, 159–74. New York: Routledge, 2020.

Kocher, Paul. "Middle-earth: An Imaginary World?" In *Understanding* The Lord of the Rings: *The Best of Tolkien Criticism,* edited by Rose A. Zimbardo and Neil D. Isaacs, 146–62. Boston: Houghton Mifflin, 2004.

Larson, Jeremy. Review of *Arda Inhabited: Environmental Relationships in* The Lord of the Rings, by Susan Jeffers. *Mythlore* (Sept. 22, 2015): 171–76.

Le Guin, Ursula K. "Prophets and Mirrors: Science Fiction as a Way of Seeing." *The Living Light* 7, no. 3 (Fall 1970): 110–21.

Light, Andrew. "Tolkien's Green Time: Environmental Themes in *The Lord of the Rings*." In *The Lord of the Rings and Philosophy*, 150–63. Chicago: Open Court, 2003.

Mack, Robert L. "Voice Lessons: The Seductive Appeal of Vocal Control in Frank Herbert's *Dune*." *Journal of the Fantastic in the Arts* 22, no. 1 (2011): 39–59.

Mellamphy, Nandita Biswas. "Terra-&-Terror Ecology: Secrets from the Arrakeen Underground." *Design Ecologies* 3, no. 1 (2013): 67–91.

Mendlesohn, Farah. *Rhetorics of Fantasy*. Middletown, CT: Wesleyan Univ. Press, 2008.

Morton, Timothy. "Imperial Measures: *Dune*, Ecology, and Romantic Consumerism." In *Romanticism on the Net* 21 (2001). https://doi.org/10.7202/005966ar.

Noel, Ruth S. *The Languages of Tolkien's Middle-earth*. Boston: Houghton Mifflin, 1980.

O'Connor, Flannery. *The Complete Stories*. New York: Farrar, Straus and Giroux, 1971.

O'Reilly, Timothy. *Frank Herbert*. New York: Frederick Ungar, 1981.

Otto, Eric C. *Green Speculations: Science Fiction and Transformative Environmentalism*. Columbus, OH: Ohio State Univ. Press, 2012.

Oziewicz, Marek. *One Earth, One People: The Mythopoeic Fantasy Series of Ursula K. Le Guin, Lloyd Alexander, Madeleine L'Engle, and Orson Scott Card*. Jefferson, NC: McFarland, 2008.

Pak, Chris. *Terraforming: Ecopolitical Transformations and Environmentalism in Science Fiction*. Liverpool: Liverpool Univ. Press, 2016.

Palumbo, Donald E. "The Monomyth and Chaos Theory: 'Perhaps We Should Believe in Magic.'" *Journal of the Fantastic in the Arts* 12, no. 1 (2001): 34–76.

———. "The Monomyth as Fractal Pattern in Frank Herbert's Dune Novels." *Science-Fiction Studies* 25, no. 3 (1998): 433–58.

———. "'Plots within Plots . . . Patterns within Patterns': Chaos-Theory Concepts and Structures in Frank Herbert's Dune Novels." *Journal of the Fantastic in the Arts* 8, no. 1 (1997): 55–77.

Parkerson, Ronny. "Semantics, General Semantics, and Ecology in Frank Herbert's *Dune*." *ETC: A Review of General Semantics* 55, no. 3 (1998): 317–28.

Phillips, Michael. "'The Greatest Predator Ever Known': The Golden Path and Political Philosophy as Ecology." In *Discovering Dune*, edited by Dominic J. Nardi and N. Trevor Brierly, 46–63. Jefferson, NC: McFarland, 2022.

Prieto, Eric. "Geocriticism Meets Ecocriticism: Bertrand Westphal and Environmental Thinking." In *Ecocriticism and Geocriticism*, edited by Robert T. Tally Jr. and Christine M. Battista, 19–35. New York: Palgrave Macmillan, 2016.

Prieto-Pablos, Juan A. "The Ambivalent Hero of Contemporary Fantasy and Science Fiction." *Extrapolation* 32, no. 1 (1991): 64–80.

Reef, Paul. "From Taming Sand Dunes to Planetary Ecology: Historical Perspectives on Environmental Thought and Politics in the Dune Saga. In *Discovering Dune*, edited by Dominic J. Nardi and N. Trevor Brierly, 156–76. Jefferson, NC: McFarland, 2022.

Royston, Edward John. "*Dune* and the Metanarrative of Power." In *Discovering Dune*, edited by Dominic J. Nardi and N. Trevor Brierly, 13–28. Jefferson, NC: McFarland, 2022.

Rueckert, William. "Literature and Ecology: An Experiment in Ecocriticism." In *The Ecocriticism Reader,* edited by Cheryll Glotfelty and Harold Fromm, 105–23. Athens: Univ. of Georgia Press, 1996.

Senior, William A. "Frank Herbert's Prescience: *Dune* and the Modern World." *Journal of the Fantastic in the Arts* 17, no. 4 (Winter 2007): 317–20.

Shippey, Tom. *J. R. R. Tolkien: Author of the Century.* Boston: Houghton Mifflin, 2000.

———. *The Road to Middle-earth.* Boston: Houghton Mifflin, 2003.

Simonson, Martin, ed. *Representations of Nature in Middle-earth.* Zurich and Jena: Walking Tree Publishers, 2015.

Stephenson, Neal. *Snow Crash.* New York: Del Rey, 2000.

Stratton, Susan. "The Messiah and the Greens: The Shape of Environmental Action in *Dune* and *Pacific Edge.*" *Extrapolation* 42, no. 4 (2001): 303–16.

Tally, Jr., Robert T., and Christine M. Battista, eds. *Ecocriticism and Geocriticism.* New York: Palgrave Macmillan, 2016.

Tolkien, J. R. R. "On Fairy-Stories." In *The Monsters and the Critics and Other Essays,* edited by Christopher Tolkien, 109–61. Boston: Houghton Mifflin, 1984.

———. *The Fellowship of the Ring.* New York: Del Rey, 2012.

———. *The Letters of J. R. R. Tolkien.* Edited by Humphrey Carpenter. Boston: Mariner, 2000.

———. *The Return of the King.* New York: Del Rey, 2012.

———. *The Two Towers.* New York: Del Rey, 2012.

Touponce, William F. *Frank Herbert.* Boston: Twayne, 1988.

Tyler, J. E. A. *The Tolkien Companion.* Bexley, OH: Gramercy, 2000.

Warren, Karen J., and Barbara Wells-Howe, eds. *Ecological Feminism.* London: Routledge, 1994.

INDEX

Arda Inhabited (Jeffers), 28, 59. *See also* Jeffers, Susan

Beowulf, 41, 44, 92
bioregionalism, 28, 62
Bombadil, Tom, 67–8, 69, 73, 120
Brawley, Chris, 5, 10, 19, 20–25, 40, 47–48, 132, 133

Catholicism, 2, 105, 114, 116, 122
Children of Dune (Herbert), 14, 126
Clark, Timothy, 5, 16
Curry, Patrick, 5, 13–14, 28–29, 39, 48, 61, 62, 135, 137

Dickerson, Matthew T., 28, 42, 46, 58–59, 61, 93, 123. See also *Ents, Elves, and Eriador* (Dickerson & Evans)
Donahue, Brian, 61, 65
Dreamer of Dune (Brian Herbert), 101
Dune Chronicles (Herbert), 14, 93, 134
Dune Messiah (Herbert), 37, 125

ecocriticism, 5–6, 13–18, 21–24, 26–27, 32, 64, 124
Ents, Elves, and Eriador (Dickerson & Evans), 28, 58–59

Evans, Jonathan, 28, 42, 46, 58–59, 61, 93, 123. See also *Ents, Elves, and Eriador* (Dickerson & Evans)

The Faerie Queene (Spencer), 96
The Fellowship of the Ring (Tolkien), 28, 30, 45
Flieger, Verlyn, 87, 89, 90–92

Garrard, Greg, 5, 27, 39, 43
God Emperor of Dune (Herbert), 44, 70

Herbert, Brian, 73, 101, 120, 129, 135

Jeffers, Susan, 28, 31, 59, 61, 64, 88, 90–91, 93, 116, 118, 126

Kennedy, Kara, 94–95

Le Guin, Ursula K., 5, 11
Lewis, C. S., 15, 19, 47, 67, 64, 88, 90–91, 93, 128

The Maker of Dune (Herbert), 97

"On Fairy-Stories" (Tolkien), 6–7, 11, 19, 37, 40

163

O'Reilly, Timothy, 65–66, 96, 108
Oziewicz, Marek, 5, 7, 8, 9, 15, 20, 85, 113, 132, 133, 136,

The Return of the King (Tolkien), 51, 119

Shippey, Tom, 87, 88
The Silmarillion (Tolkien), 29, 46–47, 63-64, 78, 79, 90

Through the Language Glass (Deutscher), 100

Touponce, William F., 95–96, 99–100, 106, 108–12
The Two Towers (Tolkien), 10, 49, 52–3, 55, 67–68, 83

Williams, Charles, 82, 128

Zen Buddhism, 2, 93, 123